HOW THE SPIRITUAL
WORLD PROJECTS
INTO PHYSICAL EXISTENCE

The Influence of the Dead

HOW THE SPIRITUAL WORLD PROJECTS INTO PHYSICAL EXISTENCE

The Influence of the Dead

Ten lectures given in various cities between 12 January and 23 December 1913

ENGLISH BY ANNA R. MEUSS

INTRODUCTION BY MARGARET JONAS

RUDOLF STEINER

RUDOLF STEINER PRESS

CW 150

The publishers gratefully acknowledge the generous funding of this publication by the estate of Dr Eva Frommer MD (1927–2004) and the Anthroposophical Society in Great Britain

Rudolf Steiner Press
Hillside House, The Square
Forest Row, RH18 5ES

www.rudolfsteinerpress.com

Published by Rudolf Steiner Press 2014

Originally published in German under the title *Die Welt des Geistes und ihr Hereinragen in das physische Dasein, Das Einwirken der Toten in die Welt der Lebenden* (volume 150 in the *Rudolf Steiner Gesamtausgabe* or Collected Works) by Rudolf Steiner Verlag, Dornach. Based on transcripts and notes (not reviewed by the speaker) edited by Hendrik Knobel. This authorized translation is based on the latest available (third) edition, 1980

Published by permission of the Rudolf Steiner Nachlassverwaltung, Dornach

A catalogue record for this book is available from the British Library

ISBN 978 1 85584 404 9

Cover by Mary Giddens
Typeset by DP Photosetting, Neath, West Glamorgan
Printed and bound in Great Britain by Gutenberg Press Ltd., Malta

CONTENTS

significance of the sense of hearing in dream life. Sense for music, rhythm and harmony. The significance of the senses of self-perception for life after death. Connection between the living and the dead. The significance of supersensible ideas for the experience of sleep and as food for the dead. The condition in which the dead are if they lack this food. Earthly mission to awaken spiritual ideas.

LECTURE 4
ERFURT, 13 APRIL 1913 (EVENING)

Establishing a new branch. The name of the new branch. Influence of the dead on the world of the living. Raphael and how his father influenced him. Example from Rudolf Steiner's work as a teacher. The spiritual connection with the dead and today's industrial environment. Raphael's *School of Athens*. Paul as the main figure in the painting and the misrepresentations of this fact. Anthroposophy as earthly fruit. The continued influence of the dead to help civilization to progress by influencing the world of the living.

LECTURE 5
PARIS, 5 MAY 1913

The concept of number. Microcosm and macrocosm. Transformation of the soul's power with initiation. Thinking separating off, out-of-body experience. The idea of love. Separation of the power of speech, perception of the word's spiritual power, of life before birth and humanity's development. Separation of the blood forces with the will meditation. Embodiments on earth and life between death and rebirth. The connection with the dead. Experience of immortality in the human being.

LECTURE 6
STOCKHOLM, 8 JUNE 1913

Goethe's words on nature and spirit in *Faust*. The earth as a living whole. Man and earth, waking and sleeping. Kepler's, Giordano Bruno's and Goethe's view of the earth. Why people may die young. Nature and spirit in human beings, in men and women. Nature and spirit as an alternating state, not opposite. The three entities essential nature, spirit and nature.

LECTURE 10

LEIPZIG, 12 JANUARY 1913

Modern life—economics, philosophy of life and religious life. The nature of public opinion. Jatho movement, Ostwald. Mephistopheles and Faust. Influences in history. Heraclitus. Florence in the late Middle Ages. Subordinate luciferic spirits creating public opinion. Monads and the many different spiritual entities. Potential for going astray because of Lucifer and Ahriman.

pages 105–107

INTRODUCTION

These lectures were given by Rudolf Steiner to members of the Anthroposophical Society in various European cities in 1913. In February of that year he had founded the Society, which had separated off from the Theosophical Society within which he had led the German Section. The split was mainly over the declaration by Annie Besant and leading theosophists that the young Krishnamurti was a reincarnation of Jesus Christ. From Steiner's spiritual research it was clear to him that Christ entered a human body once and once only. Krishnamurti's later repudiation and departure from the Theosophical Society was to vindicate this. The turmoil surrounding this split was probably one reason why, in several of these lectures, Steiner drew attention to the machinations of the adversary powers, referred to as Lucifer and Ahriman, and how they seek to distort and mislead.

It was Steiner's custom to travel to European cities and lecture there, and this activity increased as, in many of them, a newly formed branch of the Anthroposophical Society, or a new national society, had arisen and he was asked to inaugurate it. These offshoots were often named (and this is still the custom in some countries) after a notable being—human or divine. Thus the Erfurt branch chose the name John-Raphael (Johannes-Raffael) in honour of the individuality of John the Baptist and his later incarnation which Steiner revealed as Raphael. He has significant remarks to make about Raphael's painting *The School of Athens*. In Bochum the members chose the name of the Norse god Vidar, the youngest of the Aesir (from the Norse pantheon), who survives Ragnarok (*Götterdämmerung—The Twilight of the Gods*), and avenges the death of his father Odin by destroying the materializing adversary in the form of the Fenris Wolf. Vidar is the herald of a new revitalizing age. Steiner also conjures up images of the fierce northern elemental weather beings—our thoughts and feelings are like these capricious beings, he reminds us. The

Bochum members are further praised for founding a branch in a modern industrial city and not in some rural idyll where people try to 'go back to nature'. Rudolf Steiner wanted anthroposophy to reach out into the modern world as widely as possible, as a force for change, and not to be the preserve of a favoured elite.

In several of these lectures we find reference to life after death, our relationship to the dead and how they may be reached in a non-mediumistic way. It is very noticeable that for about two years *preceding* the outbreak of the First World War, Steiner gave a number of significant lectures on this theme. He was clearly aware that, in addition to more obvious political moves, certain occult streams were determined to bring about a major war (see his lectures *The Karma of Untruthfulness*, 2 volumes, CW 173 and 174) and that a tragic loss of life probably could not be averted. Further to the activities of the adversaries Lucifer and Ahriman, he warns his listeners about another harmful effect—that on young children; especially, for instance, if they are encouraged to criticize adults too early in their development (a habit that has greatly increased since his time), they display an undesirable precociousness. If people cannot recognize Lucifer after death, he will have the effect of 'vampirizing' them. We may wonder if the current enthusiasm for 'vampire' material is some sort of reflection of this experience. In contrast, we should not see ageing and losing our teeth as something disagreeable or preventable. The longer someone can stay alive is a victory over Ahriman's activity. Nonetheless, these two powers also play a necessary role in earth evolution.

Several lectures around the Christian festivals are included: at Easter Rudolf Steiner spoke of the inevitable declining of the earth's forces, which people perceive and lament, as being replaced by the power of Christ as a counteraction to increasing materialization. At Christmas we are reminded that we are now in the autumn and winter time of the earth's evolution and not just in a seasonal event. Human beings are called on to be strong and not only to indulge in simple piety, but to find new forces within themselves as they grasp the more complicated concepts of spiritual science. The sun's victory over the earth, which used to be felt at the winter solstice, gives us hope of a future spiritual 'summertime' at the conclusion of earth evolution.

The only lecture here that was ever published as a booklet in English (though most of them have appeared in members' newsletters), discusses the painting in the Composanto cemetery at Pisa, later called *The Triumph of Death*, and Steiner, having reminded the audience that the Crusaders brought back soil from the Holy Land to Composanto, speaks of the painting as revealing great secrets of evolving humanity. Other themes touched upon are how spirit and nature interact, understanding microcosm and macrocosm—for instance in sleeping and waking; the power of meditation; that, on the whole, women find it easier to absorb spiritual truths than men; and that an incarnation lasting for perhaps only a few days, though a tragedy for the parents, may bear great importance for the soul concerned—in other words learning not to judge everything by earthly standards. Members are also admonished not to speak too casually about spiritual matters in general conversation—one wonders what he would say to this now, with the internet rife with casual and cheap remarks. Neither does Steiner encourage proselytizing. All anthroposophical endeavours should come from the heart.

As stated in the notes, the original shorthand records are imperfect in places and there is some repetition of content, but there is a wealth to be gained nonetheless, as we see themes light up which Steiner would develop much more fully later on, such as the nature of the senses—here he is just beginning to go beyond the usual five. Much more would follow in the years ahead on reincarnation and karma, elemental beings, on language and the importance of speech, the developing child, and the meaning of Christ's descent to the earth, death and resurrection—which he referred to collectively as 'the Mystery of Golgotha'. Although given to members whom he assumed already to have a basic understanding of anthroposophy, these lectures have an immediacy and provide intriguing glimpses of the great themes with which he would continue to be occupied until his death, and which he was so anxious to present not only to Europeans of 1913 but to future souls.

Margaret Jonas, September 2014

LECTURE 1

GIVING a public anthroposophical lecture at the present time—and what I am saying here must also be taken into account with anything anthroposophical that we present to the world outside, to people who have not joined an anthroposophical association—we must always be aware that the souls of people today do have a great, deep-down longing for anthroposophy but that in the parts of their inner life which they themselves are aware of there is very little connection with the spiritual truths. Of course this does not mean that one should consider what such people might like or not like in a public lecture. We should never ask ourselves about this, but we have to take into account that habits of thinking exist in our age, ways of seeing things, which in many respects are the absolute opposite of the things we must work towards in gaining anthroposophical insight. I always take great care to take into account what must be taken note of as I try to establish the difference in tone needed for a public lecture as distinct from speaking to our anthroposophical friends. And we should get in the habit of really maintaining this difference. Perhaps people who are still far from familiar with anthroposophy will not like what is said to them, but we need not take this for something undesirable providing we are aware that we have presented things to them which their souls need at that time. But when we are amongst ourselves, as it were, we truly must endeavour to go more and more deeply into things. Certain truths that are indeed extraordinarily important and significant for the present time, truths we must deal with amongst ourselves so that from that point they penetrate more and more deeply into the cultural life of the times, cannot yet be put openly and plainly before the general public.

This is something we must properly understand. Let us assume we talk of something which plays into human life all the time, of the way in which all human life on earth is penetrated by the ahrimanic, by the luciferic powers, or we talk of certain things that relate to the life between death and rebirth. We need to avoid talking too freely of these things to people who are not prepared, but not because of something that often comes up particularly in a society like ours, something we might call a degree of mystery-mongering, with most of the people involved not even having a real idea as to why this is going on. What should prevent us from talking too freely about these things to people who are not prepared is that people who are not prepared are unable to be really serious about these things, and do not consider them in sufficient depth. For anthroposophists the terms 'ahrimanic', 'luciferic powers' should gradually become something of such significance in life, something that touches them so deeply in their feelings and sentience when spoken that one gets this feeling that when we throw these words at someone unprepared the inner strength that should come when they are said has been taken from them, and we also harm ourselves if we use these terms without much thought, just when we feel like it in ordinary life. When we open our purse, for instance, and have to do with money, it is perfectly true that we are dealing with ahrimanic powers. But it is not good to use the term 'ahrimanic' without much ado any time we like, for this deadens us in our sentience, our feelings, and we then do not have the least possibility of still having words which, when we think or speak them, have the elemental, significant meaning for us which they should have. It is extraordinarily significant that we do not fling such things about in everyday life, for this will indeed gradually deprive us of the best thing, the most effective thing that anthroposophy has to offer. The more we have the anthroposophical terms on our lips under everyday conditions, the more do we deprive ourselves of the possibility that anthroposophy becomes something for us that truly sustains the soul, enters deeply into our soul. We need only consider the force of habit and we shall see that there is a difference if we use words such as 'aura', let us say, or 'ahrimanic powers' or 'luciferic powers' with a certain sense of awe, knowing that we are speaking of other worlds. If we always feel that we have to stop, as it were, before we use such words, using them only when it really is a matter for us of considering our relationship to the supersensible world, it will be something different from talking of these things of the higher world on any occasion in everyday life, having words that are taken from those worlds on our lips all the time.

I had to give this introduction because in this particular session we want to refer to something in the human soul which should always be there in our conscious mind but which we only consider in the right way if we do so with a certain sense of awe. Take the essay *The Education of the Child in the Light of Anthroposophy*.[1] There it is shown, as it were, what happens as the human being develops through seven-year periods. It is shown that up to the seventh year, to second dentition, we mainly have to do with physical body development, and in the next period, from the seventh to the 14th year, up to sexual maturity, with development of the ether body, and so on. When you consider the way the human being develops in seven-year periods you are mainly dealing with the things that the 'normal' spirits of the higher hierarchies are causing to happen in human evolution. It is indeed forward-moving development in seven-year periods, and we are able to say: The divine and spiritual powers that are truly forward-moving guide and govern this evolution in seven-year periods. If they alone were involved in human development, the whole of human life would take a different course than it actually does. Above all people would relate in a very different way to young children. They would always have the feeling that a spiritual entity was speaking in the young child. Indeed we would always feel that in everything they do, undertake, young children are receiving their impetus, their impulses, from higher worlds. And people certainly would not feel anything other but that children are acting on far higher impulses than those which they themselves are able to penetrate with their intellect. And that would continue for a relatively long time.

And people would then feel that the last thing they want is for children to be really clever in the human and earthly sense as early as possible, something which people today consider highly desirable. If people only had children whose development was guided in seven-year periods by forward-moving divine and spiritual powers and if these people met a child who today delights people around him because he is saying and doing such clever things, whereas they would be used to those other conditions, those people would say: 'Oh, how soon has this child become godforsaken!' Things that delight people today would then be felt to be a punishment. And they would consider a young person of 15 who was as clever as he would be expected today to be utterly godforsaken. For the forward-moving divine and spiritual powers really only ask that human beings bring out their I nature completely between the 21st and 28th years. Before that anything they did would rather appear to be such that higher spiritual, supersensible impulses were acting through them. Those children would, however, have a life that would appear dreamy on the outside; but people would feel that this dreamy life was God's or the spirits' blessing, and they would not in the least desire to bring up their children in some way to be precocious in the modern sense.

We know that something else also comes into these periods of human development. As we have made clear on a number of occasions, it is the development of self-awareness in the third, fourth and fifth year, at a time which we may in general terms characterize by saying: It is the point in time to which people's memory goes back in later life. It is the moment when a person begins to say 'I' to himself or herself. You really need to see the whole development of the human being as being two streams: evolution, with the forward-moving divine and spiritual powers working on this, and then the other stream through which human beings begin to develop self-awareness, a memory that will later allow them to remember back to that moment. This does not at all come from the divine and spiritual powers. They would keep us rather dreamy for much longer, would influence the world through us. We gain self-awareness so early and say 'I' to ourselves so early merely because of the influence of the luciferic powers. We are therefore dealing with two streams—a divine and spiritual stream that is the regular one, as it were, but would only take us to a clear, definite self-awareness between our 21st and 28th years, and a luciferic stream within us. The impulses of this luciferic stream run right across the other stream, doing something completely different to what the forward-moving divine and spiritual powers really want to have from us. The effect is that actually within the first period we learn to say 'I' to ourselves, learn to develop egoity inwardly in the soul and have a memory that goes back.

If we really think about this we can get an idea of this ongoing development of ours. Think the luciferic influence away and consider only how the forward-moving spirits would make of the human being a quietly flowing stream. Think of this as an image of the ongoing flow of a human life under the influence of what are really good divine spirits. And we walk along the quietly flowing water for a bit, and then pour in red or blue matter, a chemical that will not mingle with the clear water, a second stream which from a given point onwards flows along beside the first stream. This is how the luciferic stream has been flowing in us together with the steady Yahweh or Christ stream from about the middle of our first seven-year period. Lucifer thus lives in us. If this Lucifer did not live in us we would not have that second stream. But if we lived only in the first stream, we would be aware that until we are in our twenties we really are a member of the divine and spiritual powers. Awareness of independence, of inner individuality and personal nature comes to us with the second stream. We therefore also see the wisdom of letting this luciferic stream enter into us.

Something also happens in the second seven-year period which in a sense we may consider to be a stream that is not connected with the divine spirits that are merely forward-moving. We have already referred to it from a particular point of view. It comes in about the ninth or tenth year, which is in the second seven-year period. For thoughtful individuals it brings experiences of the kind I have spoken of, giving the example of Jean Paul.[2] It probably came a bit earlier in his case, and for others it comes in about the ninth or tenth year. This is a marked strengthening, densification we might say, of the sense of self, of I. The fact that something special is happening may also be established in another way, though I would not recommend making this other way a particular rule in bringing up children. All one can say is that one can observe it when it should happen of its own accord, as I might put it, but we certainly should not play around with it, and definitely not make it a principle in bringing up children. For if you ask a child in his or her ninth or tenth year who has no clothes on to look at himself or herself in a mirror, and the child has not been dulled by our principles for bringing up children, which are often peculiar today, she or he will quite naturally feel afraid on seeing his or her unclothed figure, a certain fear, unless the child has already been made coquettish by looking in a mirror too often. We can observe this especially in children with natural feelings who have not often looked in the mirror. For this is a time when something grows in human beings that is like a kind of counterbalance to the luciferic stream that had come in the first seven-year period. In this second period, in around the ninth or tenth year, Ahriman takes hold of the human being, and his stream is a kind of counterbalance to the luciferic stream. Now we can do something that will really please Ahriman by developing the growing child's intellect, an intellect focusing on the outside world which is perceived through the senses, at this particular time, saying to ourselves: At this time the child must as far as possible be trained to form his own, independent opinion everywhere. You know that I am here referring to a principle that is fairly generally applied in education today. It is almost generally demanded today that independent judgement be developed, especially at this age. People even provide calculators so that the children are not even asked to learn their tables by heart. This is entirely so because people are, in a sense, well disposed towards Ahriman in our time. The wish is, unconsciously of course, to educate children in such a way that Ahriman can be cultivated as much as possible in the human soul. And with regard to current methods of education we say to ourselves as occultists: The people who represent these methods of education are simply bunglers. Ahriman would do better if he were to write these principles of education himself. But the things said particularly about children's independence, their own opinions, are truly based on being disciples of Ahriman. The situation, which I can only refer to briefly, will get very much worse in the immediate future. For Ahriman will be a good leader for the outer powers and guides of the spirit of our time.

Take a matter like the one we have just been discussing. We have to regard it to be something which is coming to human beings quite naturally and as a matter of course—that people feel Lucifer and Ahriman approaching them. It would be quite wrong to think that it would be better to eliminate Lucifer and Ahriman altogether. That would be quite impossible. The following will perhaps show you how impossible it would be. If our lives were not regulated, as it were, by the forward-moving divine and spiritual powers working together with the ahrimanic and luciferic powers, that is, if only the forward-moving powers were to work on us, we would gain a degree of independence at a much later time, and even this independence would be such that, just as we now perceive colours, light, we would then have no doubt at all but that divine and spiritual powers are truly at work behind the colours and the light, that is, behind the things we outwardly perceive. We would perceive world thoughts together with our sensory perceptions. We would gain independence, but only in our twenties, but we would then also perceive world thoughts out there. We would dream away our youth, for divine and spiritual powers would be active in us, and when they ceased to be active from within they would come to us from outside. We would perceive their thoughts from outside in the same way as we are now receiving sensory perceptions. We would therefore never have proper independence except for a few years towards the twentieth year, when we would be visible to ourselves. As children we would be dreamers; in the middle years we would not really be able to determine our own lives out of our own impulses and decisions, but would simply see what we have to do wherever we came face to face with the outside world (similar to the way people were still able to do in ancient Atlantis). Independence flows into us because Lucifer and Ahriman are at work in us.

Tremendously much will of course depend on it that we do not say the things foolish educationists are saying about the human being today, always talking of 'development', that one is meant to draw out the inner qualities of people. When it comes to education, we are only talking sensibly about the human being if we know that three principles are involved in the human soul, namely the forward-moving, good divine spirits, and Lucifer and Ahriman—and if we can tell these latter two apart. It is particularly valuable for us to take first of all the main point of view, from the position of the forward-moving divine spirits, and above all consider: What is asked of us, if we consider the seven-year periods in human development? With regard to this we can truly help every individual by having the right attitude. We will do something that is good for the child, whatever the circumstances, if we create situations in the first seven years where the child lives in an environment that is healthy for his or her physical body. We do something that is good for them, whatever the circumstances, by creating good authorities in the best sense of the word around children in the second seven-year period, so that they will not be know-alls at that time but rely on people around them whom they respect as authorities, people to whom they are devoted. We do something that is good when we raise children who do not want to know everything themselves in their ninth or tenth year, but who if asked why one thing or another is right and good will say: because my father, or my mother has said that it is good, or because my teacher says so. If we raise the children so that the adults around them are the accepted authorities, we do something that is good for them, whatever the circumstances.

We are doing something that is bad for the young person, whatever the circumstances, if we sin against these seven-year periods, creating such conditions that at this very time the children start to criticize the people who have the natural authority, if we do not prevent this critical attitude from developing. And we are also doing nothing particularly good for them if we do not find opportunity to talk to a person between the 14th, 15th and 21st year in such a way that one is able quite naturally to rise with him to ideals, ideals that fill the heart with joy. We have to talk about ideals with people of that age, about what life will bring for human beings who are developing in the right way, whatever the circumstances. We would be right to say: Truly our hearts might sometimes break today when 18-year-old boys, sorry, persons, are already writing for features supplements in the papers. If instead of accepting these things of theirs one were to talk with them about something which absolutely does not yet leave its mark on outer life but which they will only bring to realization later in life, if one were to talk with them about the great ideals in human life, sharing their enthusiasm, that would be the right attitude to have. Someone, an editor for instance, who accepts an article from someone who has not yet reached his 20th year is really doing something worse, whatever the circumstances, than someone who says to the young person coming in with his article: 'Now look, that is really very good what you have done. But you will have very different ideas about it when you are ten years older. So put it away for now and take it up again in ten or twelve years.' Someone who does this, and then looks at the manuscript and talks with the young person about the ideals for life which one may connect with it, is doing something which is good for the young person.

This is merely to highlight that the things said in my *The Education of the Child* essay[3] should really always be taken into account in the upbringing, whatever the circumstances. All the other things important to Lucifer and Ahriman do not permit general rules; they are indeed different for every individual, for they relate directly to the nature of the individual. There it is often a matter of the educator's tactfulness, and one can't come in with all kinds of pedantic rules. I wanted to characterize for you all that is to be found in the human soul, and how we must take Lucifer and Ahriman into account if we want to understand the whole of human nature, and we truly want to consider everything about which we should not just say: 'We have to fight Lucifer and Ahriman.' If we want to fight Lucifer, whatever the circumstances, there would be a sure way of doing this. We merely have to prevent the individual from developing memory. For just as it is true that certain Moon spirits have been brought into our evolution on earth, so it is true that memory is always a luciferic power. All we would have to do, therefore, would be not to develop a memory. This is why I said in the essay that the period between the seventh and 14th year is when it is right to develop memory. During the period before that we need not systematically train memory for there it develops of its own accord since Lucifer is most of all in human beings at that time. After second dentition, however, we start to develop memory. By then Ahriman has created his counterbalance to Lucifer, and we'll no longer play downright into Lucifer's hands when we develop our memory.

We certainly should never think of fighting Ahriman. Once again there would be a simple way of combating the worst ahrimanic influences, but it would not be good for us. What we should have to do is to knock out the teeth someone has developed at second dentition, for there we have the most striking ahrimanic influences. Human beings have only their milk teeth from the forward-moving powers. The independent dentition people have for the rest of their life is entirely due to the ahrimanic influence.

We have to see, from looking at these things, that much that is part of us cannot be part of us in any other way than having the ahrimanic and luciferic powers in us. We sometimes even manage to be quite dissatisfied with the way we unconsciously act against Ahriman. We do prepare ourselves in the course of life to have certain powers once we have gone through death, so that Ahriman will not be able to do too much to us between death and rebirth. But sometimes we allow ourselves to be quite clearly aware that the fight against Ahriman is not actually welcome, for instance when we regret the loss of every one of our teeth. Yet every time we lose a tooth we gain a power for which we have good use. Of course, I am not saying anything against fillings, or the re-implantation of teeth, for this does not add anything ahrimanic—at most the gold itself, but that does not matter. So we cannot say that it is something bad. The fact that we gradually lose our ahrimanic teeth is due to the fact that in the course of evolution we do also gain certain impulses and these overcome Ahriman. Irrespective of whether we have a tooth re-implanted or not, we have gained an impulse that helps us with the powers we need to develop at the very lowest level between death and rebirth. It is a very little thing at first, but it can show us how essentially we must truly get in the habit, as we approach reality and look beyond unreality and the great illusion that is usually around us, of seeing things in life in a very different way from the way in which they are usually seen. The weakness of old age, for example, is also a power that comes to us directly when we are sentient of it, so that once again we have something to fight Ahriman when we have gone through the gate of death. Here, between birth and death, we may indeed be annoyed if we age too soon, but with regard to our intentions after death when we want to cope with Ahriman we must be glad that we do age.

Now you see how marvellously it is arranged that the inner core of spirit and soul remains for us which has to do with the forward-moving powers as it continues to develop between birth and death. For this seed, which goes through the gate of death, is governed solely by the forward-moving powers at the point where it has developed its greatest inner resilience. The part outside this, which outwardly withers away, is where the ahrimanic powers are. And we must now consider what this Ahriman actually is to the seer.

When our plants grow from the ground, wither as autumn approaches and the leaves fall, the elemental spirits whom Ahriman sends to the earth's surface are in evidence everywhere. He then gathers in all that is dying; he has it gathered in by his elemental spirits. When you walk through the fields in autumn and see dying nature clairvoyantly, Ahriman is extending his powers everywhere, and has his elemental messengers everywhere who bring him everything that is withering physical and etheric by nature. But we human beings are really also in a kind of autumn and winter mood all day long. Truly, the soul's summer mood exists only when the soul is asleep. It truly is the case that the sleeping human body—physical body and ether body—ranks equal with a plant; and the I and the astral body, which are outside, cast their rays back on to the physical and etheric body, acting like sun and stars and letting the powers sprout forth which we have destroyed during the day. There the vegetative life grows, and daytime thinking really exists only to get rid again of what the night lets sprout forth. When we wake up, we dart across our vegetative life just as autumn does across the plants on earth. And in our daytime waking hours we do to our physical and etheric body what winter does to the earth's vegetation, to anything by way of sprouting, shooting life which they produced in the soul's summertime, that is, in sleep during the night. When we are awake, it is winter, truly winter of the soul, and we must go to sleep if we want to have the soul's springtime. That is the way it is. And from this point of view it is really easy to see why people who do not mix at least something from the soul's summer into their daytime waking life do so easily dry out. Dry scholars, withered professor types, these are the people who do not like to accept anything unless it is in full consciousness, do not like to accept anything from the soul's summertime. They dry out, turning into out-and-out winter people. And for the seer, the whole development of human daily life is seen to be very similar to what I have just been telling you about the natural world. For when human beings develop their ordinary thoughts relating to the outside world, when they are utterly materialistic in thinking only the things that happen outwardly, their thoughts affect the brain to such an extent that this brain excretes substances which Ahriman can really do with, so that Ahriman is really accompanying waking daytime life all the time. And the more materialistic we are the more are we obsessed with Ahriman. No wonder that it is true to say that materialism has to do with fear. For if you remember the Guardian of the Threshold[4] you will be aware how fear is again connected with Ahriman.

We are meant to get the feeling that in life we are indeed face to face with complicated spiritual worlds. And what anthroposophy is meant to give us is not only that we know various things, know that there is Ahriman, Lucifer, a physical body, an ether body. That is the very least of it. What we are meant to gain from anthroposophy is a certain soul mood, a basic feeling for human life, for what really is there in the depths of the soul. And so it is necessary for us to treat the words connected with these higher things with some awe, to respect them. If we have them on our lips all the time, it will all too easily happen that their serious meaning, their dignity, is blunted.

So we see the human being between birth and death as he relates to the forward-moving spiritual powers and in a sense he is between Lucifer and Ahriman. In order that the whole development of the human being may proceed in the right way, this relationship must remain like this also between death and rebirth, except that the things which are in us between birth and death will be outside between death and rebirth. Inwardly, Lucifer has his claws in the human being from the moment to which our memory goes back. Inwardly so, for human beings know nothing of this unless they learn something of it from spiritual science and get to feel about it. Things are different after death. Lucifer makes his appearance at a particular time, just as surely as he does inwardly between birth and death, and now outwardly in the life between death and rebirth. He stands before us in his whole form there, is at our side, and we walk with him! We know little of Lucifer before we have gone through the gate of death, but we know him clearly and definitely when he is at our side between death and rebirth. It is only that awareness of this can be rather unpleasant in the present time cycle. We may thus go through the region between death and rebirth having

Lucifer at our side—there's not only something terrible about him but also something beautiful, glorious as far as his outer form goes—and realize that he is needed by the world. A time is coming more and more where people will only be able to go through life after death with Lucifer if they have already got to intuit and know the luciferic impulses in the human soul properly whilst here in life. People—and there will also be more and more of them as time goes on—who do not want to know about Lucifer, and they are probably in the majority, will know all the more of Lucifer after death. It is not only that he will be at their side, but being at their side he will be drawing on their powers of soul all the time; he will vampirize human beings. This is what people prepare for by not knowing, to be vampirized by Lucifer. With this one deprives oneself of powers for the next life, for one will be giving them over to Lucifer in a way.

Things are very much the same with regard to Ahriman. Here the situation is this. The two spirits are always present between death and rebirth, but on the one occasion one of them is more present and the other less; on the other occasion it is the other way round. We pass away, and then return again in the life between death and rebirth. Lucifer is above all at our side in the passing away, Ahriman when we move towards being born again. For Ahriman takes us back to the earth again; he is important in the second half of coming back again. And he, too, is able to do dreadful things, as it were, to the people who do not want to believe in him in their life between birth and death. He will give them too much of his powers. He confers on them something he has always to spare, the powers connected with earthly gravity that mean sickness and premature death for people, bringing all kinds of accidents that seem random into earthly existence, and so on. All this has to do with these ahrimanic powers.

In Munich I presented the subject from a slightly different point of view.[5] There I showed that after death the human soul can be the spirit who serves the powers that send sickness and death from the supersensible worlds to the sense-perceptible world. The element which makes life weak is most welcome to Ahriman, making it possible for him to weaken our lives further. But again we must not be biased in our judgement. It would be quite wrong to say: So it is very bad that

Ahriman has taken us into life and that we may have to suffer the after-effects of him in life. No, it is good, because it may well be that a sickness turns out to be something that contributes a great deal to our ascending development.

When we approach the threshold that separates the supersensible from the sense-perceptible world we must always be prepared to modify our views a little and not judge things the way we are used to judging them in the ordinary physical world. For I think you'll agree, the physical world has a superabundance of Maya. Where does the materialism in the physical world come from, that materialism where people say there is no Ahriman, there simply is no devil? Who is it who shouts loudest that there is no devil? Those who are most possessed by him. For the spirit whom we call Ahriman is enormously interested in having his existence denied by those who are most possessed by him. 'The common people never know the devil, even when they've caught him.'[6] So that is a dreadful Maya, not to believe in Ahriman, for it means that he's collared one most of all when one does not believe in him; in that case one gives him the greatest power over oneself. It is wrong, therefore, to say that monists fight the devil when they rant and rave against him. No, a materialistic and monistic gathering where people rant and rave against the devil is liable to conjure up the devil. More than the witches of old do modern materialists call up the devil, much, much more so! That is the truth and the other is Maya. So we must learn to judge things differently. Someone who goes to a monistic meeting with materialistic nuance is untruthful when he says that these people free humanity from the devil. He ought to say: I am now going to a meeting where the devil is called into human culture with all the powers that human beings have. We should really be aware that as we grow into spiritual life, as it were, we learn not only concepts and ideas, but to rethink, re-feel, and still be sensible enough when facing the outside world that we do not all the time confuse that outside world in a gushing way with the truth that exists for the supersensible worlds. When people are all the time using words that really only have a true value in the supersensible worlds they are depriving themselves of the most important thing, which is that we learn to distinguish, and not to mix up, sense-perceptible and super-sensible worlds, that we learn to use the words in their proper sense.

These are various things we wanted to refer to today when for the first time we have come together in such great numbers, with visiting friends as well, in our recently established Augsburg branch. And today, when we wanted to gather the thoughts in our souls here that shall be a help in the work done here, a serious word must also be said, like a kind of official opening for this Augsburg branch. For it will surely flourish under the guidance and direction of the Masters of Wisdom and Harmony of Sentience who serve the forward-moving spirits if the work done here harmoniously takes its place in a wider stream of spiritual work. And our visiting friends have come to join you, my dear Augsburg friends, so that today they can also be with you in developing thoughts in their souls of love and devotion for the general anthroposophic cause and for every individual in his anthroposophical strivings. In these souls something will remain that had its starting point in these meetings, having developed in these souls like a wellspring of belonging together. You, my Augsburg friends, will be working on your own again here from week to week, from time to time, but only seemingly so, only in outer spatial terms. Having so many friends join you will be the starting point for the strengthening powers that can really flow into all individual work done without our spiritual movement from all those who belong to this spiritual movement, even when we are not together with friends from some group or other in terms of space.

That is why it is so good when for once the opportunity is given for a greater number of our friends to come together with a young branch. For then the point in which they have come together in time will also be an outward sign of the kind we do need, being human, that from here on the will can truly also come again and again to us to think of the individual work done there by our friends in one place or another. And if you, my dear Augsburg friends, who have been working faithfully for some time on anthroposophy will continue the work faithfully in future, do remember that there will be friends in the world who think of you with the intention that this work be a good and true part of our whole spiritual movement. Thus we share our common membership and never lose sight of the fact that we do belong together. Let it always be clear and present in our minds, for only then will those powers truly be able to help that pertain to our genuine work, the powers of the Masters of Wisdom and the Harmony of Sentience. These powers will flit invisibly through your thoughts when you also do this our anthroposophical work here, in this town. In their anthroposophical presence and activity until now our dear Augsburg members have shown in so many ways how faithfully and truthfully they want to work with us. And because of this we are also all of us doing something important when now being together gives us the occasion to unite our thoughts in the goal that has brought us together here. May the work of our Augsburg sisters and brothers be blessed and strengthened by the powers to which we are always appealing. It is in this spirit that I call for the blessing also for this branch of the Masters of Wisdom and the Harmony of Sentience, the blessing of which I know that it is with the work when we prove ourselves worthy of it.

LECTURE 2

IT may never be known how many hearts in western Europe still feel sufficiently connected in spirit and soul with the divine and natural world that on this day, this feast of hope for the future, in this year, the thought lives in them of how this is a year when this feast of spring and hope may come as early as possible, at a time when fresh shoots are rising from the womb of Mother Earth, when the season we call spring enters into human lives. Easter Sunday—it is the first Sunday after the first full moon after the first day of spring, which is 21 March. Three dates that may at other times be relatively far apart follow one another closely this year—first day of spring the day before yesterday, spring full moon yesterday, and Easter Sunday today. For those who are gaining spiritual insight into the world, something very special is inscribed in the universe in a year such as this. For someone who endeavours to go with feeling into the spiritual secrets of the universe and the evolution of time it is right also to gain a feeling for what is meant to be inscribed in our human evolution on earth with this spring festival.

Someone who knows how the sun relates to the moon, knowing it in the way in which one can get to know it from perceiving how the combined action of sun and moon is recorded in spiritual-scientific script, will also know the deep secret connected with the Christ as earth spirit and the spirit we call Yahweh or Jehovah. Those who know the connection between sun and moon will hear in sounds that awaken understanding the Paradise legend of the Fall, with human beings led astray by Lucifer, and of the words that God spoke in judgement. Those who seek to understand some of the things written between the lines in my *Occult Science* can get a sense of the connection between the secret of sun and moon and the secret that is usually referred to as the temptation by Lucifer and the action taken by Yahweh or Jehovah.

However, today we'll concentrate more on how sun and moon, as they follow one another in their influence on the earth from this Good Friday to this Easter Saturday, present something of a question mark to the occultist, being inscribed in the spiritual universe in a deeply mysterious way. And this year the answer is that they follow one another as quickly as possible, with Easter Sunday immediately following the spring full moon's Saturday. Easter Sunday is the day of remembrance and the day of hope, the day which reflects the Mystery of Golgotha for us in symbolic form. There are secrets behind the physical, sense-perceptible natural world around us, and the unveiling of such secrets will always, in a way, take us close to the solemn Guardian of the Threshold.[7] The Easter secret is another one, and in a particular way it absolutely demands that the human soul reaches maturity before understanding it, though instinctively everyone can always make that inner offering of devotion that may fill our soul when the first day of spring is followed by the day of earth confidence and trust, the day of redemption and resurrection—Easter Sunday. When spring comes, when the sun relates to the earth in such a way that thanks to its powers the plant seeds may sprout from the womb of Mother Earth, the human soul begins to shout for joy inwardly as though in the bright light of paradise, for it knows that powers move through the cosmos that in cycle upon cycle with every new year conjure forth from the earth's womb what is needed for external life and also for the soul's life, so that human beings may follow their course from the beginning to the end of Earth evolution. When the impressions made by winter as it covers Mother Earth's soil with ice and snow, all this calls into life the thought of everything that will one day cause the earth to fall into decay in the universe, and will one day take earth into the state of frozen cosmic rigidity, so that it will no longer serve as a dwelling place for humanity. If winter calls up thoughts like these, then every new spring calls up the other thought in the human soul: Yes, earth, from your very origin you have always been given new powers of youth, of life renewing itself. It is given to you to call the soul forth again to shout for joy inwardly, but also to inward devotion. And whilst the cold cover of ice is still spread on the ground, hopeful ideas nevertheless combine in the human soul with a sense, a feeling, that the earth will still be able to sustain human beings with its powers of spring and summer, so that they will have opportunity to develop all the abilities, all the inner powers that lie within them. This is the inner, reverent jubilation in the soul at the spring equinox. It arises because the soul feels full of hope that the earth can continue, and that the earth can provide the opportunity to develop human powers to the full.

But the question no doubt also comes to the human soul: Will all powers of the sun be able to overcome all the powers of winter or at least keep them in balance? Won't winter forces perhaps act so strongly on earth that the earth has to enter into a frozen state before the human soul has completed its mission on earth? Will spring always have the strength that is needed?—a thought which perhaps does not come too easily to human souls that look only at the natural world outside, but must come more and more to souls able to go deeply into the true spirit within the universe. These souls seek to decipher the great, tremendous writing in which the secrets of the world are inscribed in the cosmos. Unlike the writing of winter's struggle with summer, another writing will then be evident to the soul, the writing inscribed in our universe— when we follow the moon in its mysterious course, how it completes its cycle invisibly and visibly. Ah, the light of the moon, it is like a mysterious letter in the world script finding its place in the original eternal creative word of earthly life. When the occultist seeks to fathom this moonlight it will at first remind him of the avenging voice of Yahweh after the temptation by Lucifer in Paradise, but then it will also remind him of the marvellous, mysterious reality of the Buddha letting his spirit go out into the cosmic universe. What is the moonlight telling us when it is present in the darkness of night just as the dream is present in a human being's sleep? The occultist learns that as much is always taken away from the powers of the active sun, from the powers of the sun that again and again renew Earth evolution, as light of the sun is shone back by the full moon. The human soul may dream its way into nights filled with the moon's magic; the occultist knows that as much of the sun's light and warmth is taken away as the full moon lets shine down on to the earth of this sunlight.

The full moon thus is the constant symbol for what is taken away from the sun. And in every spring, when the sun is once again rising into earthly life with its powers, the occultist knows that, however little may be apparent on the outside, the sun's powers are weaker with every new spring than they were in the preceding spring, and that as much has been taken away of its powers as the full moon has let shine on the earth. The full moon that comes after the spring equinox may seem mysterious to human beings, lending wings to their souls, but it is also solemnly and most seriously reminding us of the earthly and cosmic fact that the sun has lost powers with every new spring, and that human beings would never be able to achieve in their mission on earth what they would achieve if those powers were not taken from the sun. To be sentient of this puts a huge question mark into the cosmos. Sentience of this determined the attitude in their hearts for the occultists of earlier times.

They would say to themselves: 'We look up to the sun. Zarathustra[8] once made its secrets known to humanity. We look up to the moon. Its secret came to its most significant expression in the Yahweh religion. Looking at the two signs in the heavens we know that sun and moon working together means decline for the earth.' Those occultists of old would turn their eyes to a point in Earth evolution itself, the point where in the fullness of time the spirit of the sun rose from the earth itself in the body of Jesus of Nazareth. When the Christ died on the cross on Golgotha and the spirit of the Christ united with the earth, this was a cosmic event in the earth's life to create a power that would counterbalance all the powers which the moon took away from the sun as this sun was influencing the earth from the cosmos. When the Christ spirit made a human soul its dwelling place and from there spread out over the whole of earth's existence as its evolution continued, something was created that replaced those sun powers which the powers of moon are taking away all the time. And so the human soul understands its connection with the cosmos when morally and spiritually it will of its own accord add the third day, the death and resurrection on Golgotha. And when they come too close to one another, the advancing powers of the sun in the cosmos, which from their infinite goodness always want to give new life to the earth, and the harsh moon spirit which because of the Lucifer spirit and its powers must take the sun's forces away from it in so far as it is but the natural sun, the human soul is morally and spiritually able to add this third day, Easter Sunday, like the answer to the great cosmic question. They are side by side most marvellously in years like the present one.

Good Friday! This year it may particularly warn us in cosmic occult writing that in every new spring powers are taken from the sun, and that the earth might die before the human soul has developed all its powers. Full moon on Easter Saturday, a marvellous secret! Up above in the cosmos the marvellous sign, symbol of Yahweh who lets the thunder of his voice roll through Paradise when human sin makes the consequence of temptation shine out; down below on earth the symbol of the newly risen power of earth, the Christ resting in his tomb! There follows the symbol of the sun who is risen again, the sun risen again from the human soul, Easter Sunday! Let us feel this trinity in our soul, let us feel the cosmic sun, followed by the cosmic moon, followed by the moral and spiritual sun. Let us feel the symbol of this trinity in our soul, how the spirit overcomes matter, life overcomes death; let us feel something of the quality that can fill us if we are occultists of our time in the proper sense of the word, so that human beings will learn to feel in the Christ impulse that is coming to revelation more and more what must be there within them so that as human beings they find the way away from the dying earth to higher stages of evolution for the immortal human soul that proceeds to live in eternity.

LECTURE 3

WEIMAR, 13 APRIL 1913

When we consider that here in the physical world we get to know this physical world, we will of course always realize that primarily we live in this world through our physical senses, our intellect. We do, however, also live in this physical world thanks to our inner life, the thoughts that come up in us, remain in our memory as the things we remember; we live in this world thanks to our feelings and will impulses. It is perfectly understandable that for someone who has not yet considered spiritual-scientific issues more deeply it must seem quite improbable that there is also supposed to be a way of living that is completely different from that in the physical world; it is clear, after all, that initially human beings know the world only through their thinking, feeling and doing.[*] But thanks to something we call initiation, there is a very different way of living in the world, one that goes beyond the physical world. Basically it is the same kind of life as when someone goes through the gate of death, entering into the time that lies between death and rebirth.

Now we have to say that in most instances the human being wishing to form an idea whilst here in his physical body of the life between death and rebirth will inwardly be overcome by a certain fear of the great void. Let us be clear in our minds that this fear is quite natural. Just try and think yourself in a position where you would have walked rather fast and come upon a deep abyss. This would offer you nothing but a dim feeling, a sense that you simply cannot know what might happen the moment

---
[*] Alternative translation: thinking, feeling and will.

you took another step. This feeling can only come when the person has run so fast that he can no longer stop himself. He says to himself: 'You have to take the next step.' The undefined nature of the fear lives in him, and this feeling could only be compared with the feeling which is always there in the soul but we are not aware of it because our attention is focused on the physical world. This feeling says to us: 'What will happen to you when you leave everything that you are used to?' A person only has to reflect that such a thing may subconsciously live in him, and it does indeed live there, something we may put in words as: 'You cannot see or hear, for the instruments serving these activities have been taken away; nor are you able to think.' We have no clear sense of these feelings but they are there in the soul, and the human being numbs himself in a way and so skips over these feelings. As soon as it arises, something else is called to mind so that the feeling cannot come to conscious awareness. But this is not the right way to prepare ourselves; we will not be able to lift the veil that lies behind death. Let us learn today how this life of ours relates to life after death.

We do quite rightly say that we perceive the physical world through the senses. Speaking of the senses people are really only speaking of those that are of use in the physical world. They can only be used in the physical world because they are bound to the instruments that will be taken from us when we die. People always list only the five senses—sight, hearing, smell, taste and touch. None of these will serve when we have left the physical body behind. To make the transition we must include all human senses. People go wrong in the way they list the senses because they forget to include themselves. They are part of the physical world themselves and would not be able to perceive themselves in this world unless they had the senses for doing so. To begin with it is only a small number of senses by which they perceive themselves—the sense of balance, the sense of movement and the sense of life. These are just as important as the other, outer senses. What is the sense of life? You can get an idea of this if you consider the difference between hunger and satiety. If human beings did not grasp themselves inwardly they would know nothing of their own bodily nature of well-being or not being well. We must speak of the sense of life just as we do of the sense of sight.

But there is also another sense we must consider. It would be quite impossible for human beings to be aware of themselves if they were not aware of the activity in muscles and sinews. This is perception of inner mobility. It is a little obscured for us because we see ourselves with our physical eyes in the physical world. We get the right feeling of that inner perception when we move in the dark; perception of the breathing process, for instance, will then be more easily clear to us.

The sense of balance, as we call it, is something we really need. When children learn to walk and stand you can see how they gradually feel their way into this sense. We have to get used to getting a sense of walking erect. This sense even has an organ consisting of the three semicircular canals in the ear. They are at right angles to one another. People fall over when these are damaged, and the absence of a sense of balance means that the individual's inner sense of orientation has been damaged.

Moving on, we find yet other senses that can give us a kind of self-perception, but it is getting more difficult. Here we must start with something that points to a state of consciousness which is no longer quite normal. It occurs in some dreams. The following dream may come to conscious awareness. Someone is seething with anger. The choir-master has come. The dream goes into every detail and may turn into a long story. Then it changes, there's the noise of passing vehicles—the firefighters are passing. Outwardly nothing happened but the shout 'fire!'. The word does sound similar to 'choir', and that sound evokes in the soul the transition from the actually heard 'fire!', which in turn gives rise to the sum of vexing ideas in the dream. The dream moves at a terrific pace. One thinks of the individual events in linear time and because of this the dream seems to be long. You see from this the great significance of sound in the soul body, especially when it gets mixed up with ideas, when words come into it. Continuing our study of the soul we find that something quite different is really happening. People do not notice these things when in deep sleep. Something would also have happened if there had not been the shout 'fire!', but now the shout covers something up and evokes the word 'choir'. A fine veil is spun from the echoes of that word. During the day the veil is terribly thick, but the subtle ideas in the soul run alongside the daytime ideas. It is just that no note is taken of them. In a dream vision like this we are getting just a wisp of the world's events as they present themselves to the soul.

We have deliberately chosen this example because hearing, the way it is for present-day humanity, is the sense closest to the supersensible senses. We are right on the border of the supersensible world and if we were able to cast off the two words we would be able to know the actual experiences in the soul.

The example clearly shows how human beings relate to the spiritual world. But the two words are holding them back. It truly is the case that by far the greater majority of our dreams are spun from the echoes in our hearing, for an inner sense lies between hearing and thinking, a sense that has completely atrophied where modern life is concerned. It becomes active as we learn to live in the spiritual world. It lives between hearing and thinking and comes to conscious awareness when we are able to hear things that are inaudible. When a sense has been awakened for rhythmic, melodious harmony ... [Gap in text.]

When we do not get through to a sense that has significance only for the physical world we are faced with a sense of the supersensible world. In the physical world this sense has divided into the sense of hearing and the sense of forming ideas. Echoes of it arise when we arrive at a form of self-awareness. Those echoes are best when we try to develop sentience for what lives in the echoes of music and poetry. The better way, however, is to get to this from the other side. This sense has atrophied in outer, physical life.

From there it continues to where we say today: The human being gains an idea of the I. We have to be honest when it comes to this idea of the I. People say 'I' and doing so gives them a degree of inner certainty. They believe, rightly, that in saying 'I' they take hold of the I. That is rightly so. It is a kind of preparing oneself to take hold of the true higher I. There is a major problem with this taking hold; if it were not, there would not be all that philosophical endeavour to fathom it. In my *Philosophy of Spiritual Activity* I endeavoured to show how it may be fathomed. All of this is part of self-perception. You have to grasp inwardly what makes one addresses oneself as 'I'. We thus have senses for grasping the outside world and others by which we grasp our self when we hear the soundless sound.

The familiar five senses are specifically developed here in the physical world. They are of no significance for the initiate in the spiritual world. The other senses, by which human beings gain self-perception, have atrophied. These are of great significance for human beings when they go through the gate of death.

The first thing human beings need on the other side is the sense that makes the transition from external to inner musicality. The presence of the external instrument of hearing does not impede this sense. Today the ear has merely bludgeoned the sense to death. In the physical world we can perceive the power of the sense when musicians compose. The sense is then present behind the creative work. After death it becomes a sense through which human beings are directed towards their surroundings. We then live with music inwardly. After death the sense becomes an outer sense and for a time after death we perceive what passes through the world, for the world is filled with rhythmic, musical harmonies. Someone who did not perceive this rhythmic, musical harmony would be like someone in the physical world who cannot perceive the inorganic.

In my book *Theosophy* you will find under the description of devachan how life on the other side consists in the spreading of musical, rhythmic harmonies. In fact, the in-front and the at-the-back connect with the above and below, whereas we merely know, thanks to our sense of balance, that we are upright as we walk. We then perceive the spirits that are above and below, to left and right. The inner senses which are now atrophied thus spread out and convey the world of the spirit to us. Then the sense of balance changes into the sense of harmony and rhythm, then the sense of movement connects. When we are free of all muscles and sinews the sense which otherwise is concentrated by the body will spread out and we arrive at the possibility of being everywhere in the universe the way we are now in our own body thanks to the sense of movement. In the spiritual world the outside world is like the way in which a muscular movement happens in the physical world. When a hand is put out to a child, the child understands this and copies the movement. The sense of movement awakens in the inward experience of the copied movement.

As time goes on one is thoroughly cured of some theories that persistently have the problem of saying: 'We do live within us.' But there is no blood circulation in the supersensible world.

The inner sense of movement will be particularly important when we have died; the sense of life grows important for us—unless it can be applied in an unpleasant way—because we won't have headaches any more, nor feel hungry.

The senses which are atrophied here will be very much stimulated when we go through the gate of death. We are unable to perceive our own bodily nature with our own bodily nature; the eye cannot see itself and the brain cannot examine itself; an organ which perceives something therefore cannot be one that perceives itself. The sense of life, as we called it, needs to be separated out from our bodily nature and thus comes close to the soul principle. With the sense of balance it is not that it conveys the process of perception; it merely expresses itself symbolically in it.

These senses are really egotistical by nature, for human beings perceive their self through them. And we must not ignore the fact that we also take the egotistical part of us with us on departing this life. Initially we therefore retain the more egotistical part and this explains why human beings enter into a rather egotistical state immediately after death. Just as children bring their senses with them into physical existence and must first get used to the physical world perceived through the senses, so human beings who have left their bodies must get their senses used to the supersensible world. That takes quite a long time after death, and whilst they are getting their senses into the habit they are initially left only with whatever brought them together with the outside world in the physical world as a memory, and this is the less pleasant part of the memory. The first recall takes only a few days, presenting as a memory tableau, as we know. Then it begins to change so that anything which here is their inmost part connects in an inward way and the individual gets used inwardly to entering into everything he has lived through, for the possibility of sensory perception does, of course, come to an end.

A concrete example. We had some form of life partnership with another person. We die, he stays behind on the physical plane. We get more and more used to holding back something other than memory from the inner part of us. When we look at a dead person we see that he knows what we have shared with him during life on earth. Death cuts the thread and now the devastating perception may be made that one meets dead people who tell one, using the means of communication: 'I lived with this or that person. I know that he lives on, but I only know about him up to my death.' That means great pain. The dead individual now misses the living one. Because of this the dead are mainly lamenting those whom they loved and whom they now cannot reach. It needs to be made known that this is where we can do a great service to the dead by meeting them halfway. The external senses have been taken from the dead; all that lives in them now is what they experienced together with us. Yes, ordinary life really has nothing to offer that might make a difference. The situation can only be changed if bonds are created between the dead and the living. For someone who is dead it usually is as if we were looking up to them. [Gap in the text.] But there is a common bond between the dead and the living, and that is our thinking of supersensible thoughts. Spiritual thinking is this common bond.

Let me stress that we can read to the dead about supersensible worlds. When we have time we sit down and in our thoughts go through the subject matter of occult science, imagining in the liveliest possible way that the dead are with us. This removes the torment for them of thinking we're not there. We have got really good results with this in the anthroposophical movement by reading to the dead in our thoughts. They are then together with us, and this is what they need, what they long for.

There are two things connected with living with the dead. The first is what has just been said, that they miss the people they lived with on earth. We can help them here by reading to them. We need to be together with the dead and bridge the existing conditions. Now what does it mean to the dead when we read anthroposophy to them though they did not want to know about it in life? People often say this. But that is a materialistic objection, for conditions do not stay the same. It may be the case, for instance, that there are two brothers. One is inclined towards spiritual science, but the other gets more and more angry about it. He talks himself into an ever greater rage. But he is only doing this because he wants to blank out his inner longing for spiritual science. You cannot easily get through to him in life, and it is not a good thing to agitate in favour of anthroposophy. In death, the things people have longed for most will be most evident, and we can do the best possible thing for these very souls if we read to them. Someone who has been interested in anthroposophy in this life will of course continue to be interested in it on the other side. This is the one thing.

The other thing we have to consider, especially at the present time, is that when we enter into the supersensible world every day in our sleep we are in the same world as the dead. We just don't know about it any more after waking up. How do most people go to sleep? We may say that when they have crossed the threshold to sleep not much of what they have taken with them is spiritual. People who have taken alcoholic drinks to help them sleep will not bring much with them that is spiritual. But there are many nuances to this. We often hear: 'Well, what is the good of learning spiritual science when one will still not be able to look into the spiritual worlds?' Well, you need only give enough attention to it and you will also take some of it with you into sleep. Think of a sleeping city, sleeping people, their souls free of the body. Sleeping souls are something different to the spiritual world than they are to the physical world. It is something similar for the dead. The things we give to the dead, things they take into their conscious awareness, are exactly what they need for their life. And when we bring spiritual thoughts to them they have nourishment; if we don't they will be hungry, so that we may say: 'By cultivating spiritual thoughts here on earth we can provide nourishment for the dead. We can let them go hungry if we do not bring spiritual thoughts to them.' When fields lie fallow they produce no crops to feed humanity and people may die of starvation. The dead cannot die of starvation, of course, all they can do is suffer when spiritual life lies fallow on earth.

The point is that here on earth science follows various laws about particular situations, and one ideal is that life as such can be understood with the help of science. But we do not get to know life here on the physical plane. All the laws do relate to living things, but in spite of all that knowledge we cannot fathom life. When it comes to the super-sensible world, all scientific studies cannot get to know death. For someone who is able to see through things, it is nonsense to believe that there is such a thing as death in the supersensible world. There are sleeplike states of consciousness and also a longing for death, just as we would wish to understand life, but there is no death there. We should not think that we might perish in the spiritual world, and we also cannot die there. Nor can we destroy our conscious awareness there, something which corresponds to dying in this world here. But one can grow isolated in the spiritual world.

It is a matter of not being able to perceive the physical world perceived through the senses. One knows only of oneself, and nothing of others. This is known as the pain and suffering of kamaloka. The conscious awareness of human beings is broadened out by the sociable life after death, and we also enter into sociability with the different spirits in the supersensible world.

One objection that may also be raised will be resolved in Erfurt this evening. It is this: 'How come—the dead are in the supersensible world. Are they able to learn something when we read to them about the supersensible worlds?' They cannot learn about things in the supersensible world unless we give them to them from our earth. The thoughts must stream up from the earth. Human beings are on earth to get to know not just a vale of tears but also anthroposophy. People often think that one can also get to know anthroposophy after death, but that is quite wrong. Having gone through the gate of death human beings put away the things they have learned on earth.[9]

LECTURE 4

IT must be a matter of great pleasure that, with our anthroposophical work being done in different places, we are now able to come together here in Erfurt where some of our friends have been working together for some time, seeking to develop anthroposophical life, spiritual development, under conditions that sometimes go against us. And this John Raphael [Johannes Raffael] Branch is the fruit of these endeavours. Coming from outside and meeting with our Erfurt friends, and now able to dedicate this Branch, we may as an introduction turn our minds to the significance which the anthroposophical work done today has for human evolution altogether.

My friends, how do our anthroposophical branches come into existence? If one considers this they may really be said to arise in a wonderful way. For they come into flower here and there, rather like spiritual products of nature, and the people who feel called upon to establish such a branch in their enthusiasm stand there—in their feelings and through the occult power behind these feelings—like a spiritual power. They feel they have to do something. A branch is not established out of present civilization but out of the hearts of those who feel called to do this. There is nothing in our present civilization that comes to a human being and might suggest from outside, as it were, that one join in the anthroposophical work. For someone who decides to do anthroposophical work may expect very different things in furthering the work from ease and recognition. Not one of the accepted streams and endeavours of the present time seeks to win souls for anthroposophy, and anyone looking at our anthroposophical movement the way it is will confirm that it does not agitate for anthroposophy in the ordinary sense. Apart from the fact that circumstances will not permit speakers to go anywhere but where they are called, we consider the nature of the movement to be such that we will try everything to provide occasion for people to hear about it; but it is for them to come to the anthroposophical work. When one sees propaganda being made, one will see that this has nothing to do with the stream we represent, and this is how every movement basing itself on occultism should act. It should be left to people to come of their own accord. And this movement then sees anthroposophical branches coming up here and there because something is flowing into the movement which continues to act in the proper karmic order. And it mostly is the case that the branches are brought to the existing movement. We have to appreciate the fact that branches arise in spite of all the prejudice that exists. There have to be enthusiastic souls who proceed to establish such branches of their own accord.

You know we cannot count on a great and powerful effect from the beginning, and the people who are enthusiastic about our work must know that they will meet with scorn and derision. They have to know this and also that the work will initially be difficult, demanding self-denial. We have never seen anything else; people are often disappointed over and over again. Again and again public lectures are organized but we have met with failure only where we took fright at initial failures. When we took it calmly that five people came to the first lecture, none to the second, and continued the work in spite of this, we also saw success in the end. We should make ourselves independent of instantly apparent successes, for to feel encouraged by successes is easy but not to give up, that is difficult. The latter means that there is no outside prop. We find, therefore, that our branches often have to work hard from their very beginning. Misunderstanding will follow misunderstanding, but we should train ourselves to see what is right.

We have on occasion also had a different echo. I was called to a city— I won't give the name—to give lectures on two or three occasions. When there was no result the individual concerned said: 'That's enough.

Let people come and ask us to give lectures from now on.' I told him that would probably mean a long wait—and we are still waiting. I know very well that the right thing to do here is to express gratitude to our friends, seeing that they have worked so hard for many years. The friends who have come with me will feel the same gratitude. The thoughts our friends direct to this place will give strength, and we'll progress if we keep faith with one another. The main thing for spiritual work is to give support to others; the work will succeed all the better the more such support is given. I would say that this Erfurt branch has shown in an outward sign how closely it feels connected with our way of working and our approach, and this feeling of being connected will be an inner impulse for them to succeed in the work.

It is something of a risk to go into concrete details of anthroposophical research, and in a way I may call it an achievement in our work that the way our friends have come to be at home in anthroposophy has meant that individuals among us have developed a feeling that it is not just a matter of developing theories, but that the work leads to real insights. One does make the strangest discoveries particularly in these areas. Oddly enough people outside who know nothing of the anthroposophical work begin to criticize the concrete research work though they have no idea of the spiritual work that has to be done, for instance, to establish the things said in my book *The Spiritual Guidance of Man and Humanity*. They set about criticizing the way research is done in this field. Criticism is expressed about the two Jesus children, for example.[10] It may be that those people have something to say when one is dealing with general truths. But when it is a matter of something specific all one can do is stay silent. People should say to themselves: 'It does seem odd what is said there, but it is none of my business.'[11]

It is all the more valuable, however, when our Erfurt friends feel that they have a special connection with these things. For nothing is said but things that can be checked using the means at our disposal. One of those truths is that John the Baptist is the same soul as Raphael.[12, 13] I therefore feel that it is a good deed spiritually to call this branch the John Raphael Branch and so reflect a truth found in spiritual research. This also makes this ceremony an intimate one. By referring to an occult truth as we give a name we make it known that we are keeping the faith with regard to things that are for us most intimate. And then the words gain in depth which the poet Novalis wrote and which we heard here today.[14]

We must, after all, look for the most important element in the sentience and feelings that unite us. Nothing will give rise to them but the basis of our insight. Yet we must not take it easy. Insight must catch fire so that we feel ourselves to be together, and if it is in accord with our friends' intentions that I say a few words of dedication, I think it is right to say that I feel real satisfaction in saying these words; it is a dedication that comes from the heart. I may say, therefore: Let my words give an impulse to the work we have begun. You will be working under the protection of the mights and powers of which we know that they work among us unseen—the Masters of Wisdom and the Harmony of Sentience—if we do our work lovingly and faithfully. I may speak of what lived among you when out of an intimate impulse you endeavoured to give your branch a name, saying that the protective powers that watch over you and give us impulses for our work, powers of which we know that they are called the Masters of Wisdom and the Harmony of Sentience, I call upon them that the branch may flourish and be a centre in this city for the spiritual progress we long for. And with this you are given the possibility of making the connection with something of which I spoke to the friends who had come together in Weimar, making it in a particular way, though it will not matter if not everyone has heard of it before.

It has to do with the life between death and rebirth. It had been said that after leaving the physical plane an individual might have certain difficulties in connecting with those who have remained behind on earth. It may be possible that the individual who has gone through the gate of death knows of someone who has been left behind, knows of things they shared in life before he had gone through the gate of death. Something shared with someone else on earth lives on in the mind of the dead individual. But there are many cases where such a connection cannot be made, and that happens if the person left behind develops thoughts that are not spiritual by nature.

When someone who has remained behind on earth very rarely fills his soul with spiritual thoughts, the dead soul has no access to such a soul. I am speaking of the way in which a living individual may be able to connect with someone who has died.

A particular line of research provided me with remarkable information on communicating with the dead. It may seem strange at first that John the Baptist presented prophetic activity filled with will impulses to the world, and that later on this soul appeared again as Raphael, in a marvellously self-contained way wholly given to the world in deep devotion. Many things seem strange and peculiar to us in spiritual investigation. Much seems dangerous to us because it is so self-evident. And when we consider things in more depth it may come as a shock to see that many of them are not the way we thought them to be. For someone who has realized the truth of a fact like the one we are considering, that John and Raphael were identical, it is important to keep a feeling of wonder alive. I can assure those who are not able to investigate such facts for themselves that things do not come up when you are looking for them; they come unsought. To think a lot about such things does not help much at all. What helps most is to be able to wait calmly until the inspiration comes. And then it is good if one is able to be amazed, in a way, at what is given.

The straight way of the intellect is not suitable for occult research. A sense of wonder means that one will gradually come to see that something we wonder at proves understandable. Thus I realized one day that something different lived as an after-effect in Raphael's soul. His work was amazing, and I was able to see that this after-effect had actually come from his father. He had died when Raphael was just ten years old. Now the father might have lived a little longer—I am speaking hypothetically. He could have had the strength to live longer. But he took that strength with him into the spiritual world, and there are occasions when such strengths can be extremely powerful. The father had not been a great painter, but inwardly he was a painter, he lived in ideas of paintings that he could not bring to realization whilst still in a physical body. He sent those powers from the spiritual world to his son, and this is why young Raphael could turn into such a great painter. He gained his artistic abilities from the powers his father sent to him from the spiritual world. This does not, of course, make Raphael a lesser man; it has merely served to show how powers act down from the spiritual into the physical world. Lessing said a strange thing.[15] He said that Raphael would have been a great painter even if he had been born without hands. The powers that were in the Baptist John were transformed into the painter Raphael.

Life will be taken a great deal further if we are able to gain insight into the way the spiritual world influences the physical world.

I had to work as a teacher for a long time.[16] It was my task to teach children who had lost their father. If you are a conscientious teacher you have to take everything into account. You have to ask what are the inherent abilities, what is the influence of the environment, and so on. I tried to consider everything that could be outwardly considered, but a difficulty remained. I then said to myself, the father has died, and he had particular aims for his children. And things went all right once I took the father's intentions into account. The father's powers of will were there. So one sees how the dead on their part influence the realm of the living.

It has to be remembered, however, that the dead are unable to know what those who remained on earth are doing, as I also said this morning. When someone has gone through the gate of death and knows that his impulses influence the physical world, it can be painful for him that he is unable to perceive those he has left behind. The dead can feel inner discomfort when they are unable to know what is going on down there. This feeling can be removed by sending nourishment to the dead. Being in life, it is up to us to create the opportunity for the dead to perceive us. Remember that it needs a thought to ignite spiritual life, as it were, in our soul. It really is an important positive thought to know that the dead individual is there, within our reach, once they have gone through the gate of death, for that is a thought that can never come by concerning ourselves with the physical world perceived through the senses. We should be firmly convinced in our hearts that the person who has died is living.

You see, at times when there was not yet anything to cause confusion there was really no need for anthroposophy, but times change as human evolution progresses. Not long ago every individual, including those who worked with such sciences as then existed, was convinced that the dead lived. Today people are confused. This concerns not only those who doubt that the dead are present, but also the rest, and that is also the reason why anthroposophy had to come. We know that the dead live. It is the thoughts hidden deep in our souls that matter, and we often have not the least idea of them. All of us are in the midst of a mechanized age that has given us railways, ships, telegraphs and other inventions. What does it mean, for instance, to go on a tram compared to the fact that it is not all that long ago that there were no electric trams? It means that we are surrounded by things put together in a purely mechanical way. This generates an imagination, but one that may remain unconscious; it is there, however, influencing the soul and apt to deprive us of our belief in life after death. This life is torn out by its roots. That belief could still cope with the horse-drawn coaches of old, but cannot do so when it comes to modern forms of transport. These call for greater, stronger powers.

I would now refer to something which I have said on quite a few occasions.[17] Some people want to bring the anthroposophical movement to a halt. When the first railway was to be built, the faculty of medicine were asked what they thought of the project with regard to the health of travellers. The physicians were seriously concerned about running the railways and firmly advised against it. They said if one was nevertheless going to build the railways, it would be absolutely essential to put tall hoardings on either side, otherwise the rapidly changing images seen by travellers would without doubt cause concussion. But this expert opinion did not stop progress, nor will opposition put a stop to the anthroposophical movement. By the way, I did not intend to make fun of the faculty of medicine but merely wanted to say that such expert opinions cannot stop progress; it advances in the face of opposition. The railways have indeed made people more nervy, and humanity has changed because of them. The whole fabric of the inner life has changed, and without the railways people would still have greater inwardness. The experts had made their point, and they had been right.

Earth evolution proceeds in such a way that this had to happen the way it did. In anthroposophy there is no wish to turn the clock back, but it will be clear that faith could hold its own with the old coaches but not with the railways.

Anthroposophy is active in the subconscious and belief in the spiritual world will be an important factor in the further evolution of humanity. Faith is no longer sincere among very many people today. Because of this the reasons coming from anthroposophy must be brought into play. If we take note of this we will find that in earlier times people had that spiritual connection with the dead and were able to give them sufficient strength. Today it needs spiritual insight and there we see that the spiritual thought of the soul living on must be fired by insight. We are able to say that because our age has assumed a particular form it has been necessary to let anthroposophy flow in, and this stream will make it possible again for the living to feel connected with the dead. We need not be devastated at having been left behind, for we can be the helpers of the dead.

On the other hand the dead can also be our helpers. Some people know very well what they owe to the dead. Many things have come from the dead where spiritual insight is concerned, and it has always been extraordinarily important to me, for example, that the dead, especially those who had died early, were helpers. It is not always a matter of someone who has gone through the gate of death having been necessarily of outstanding intellect here on earth if he is to help the living. Young children often die who are advanced souls in the spiritual world and able to tell us a great deal. People who merely consider this intellectually will not be able to penetrate such secrets.

As I said earlier, the dead can show us one thing and another. How does that happen? Let me give you an example. I have on several earlier occasions told you how it was with Raphael's *School of Athens*.[18] The two figures at the centre are usually thought to be Plato[19] and Aristotle.[20] That is a misrepresentation, and you will not be able to make much of this significant painting if you study it the way Baedeker did, who said that individual figures represent this or that person. The one figure is actually Paul, who appeared among the philosophers in Athens.[21] I was able to understand various things when I used the Akashic Record to track down what had made Raphael paint that picture. Other investigations had convinced me about the origin of the Gospels—no connection here with the *School of Athens*. The writers of the Gospels had at times established dates according to the stars, which means that they did study astrology. This is a separate fact, and initially it does not relate to Raphael's painting. Then I had the good fortune or was given the grace that someone who had died relatively early drew my attention to the connection between the right and left sides of the painting. I was told that the words from Luke's Gospel that had originally been included in the painting had later been painted over, writing in words of the school of Pythagoras instead. Now one can also understand the gesture where on the other side compasses are used to point to astrology, and I was able to establish that Raphael had intended to show astrology on the right. And the things which were discovered there would be written down on the other side. The Gospels were thus written on the basis of astrology. Now you see, it was important to me to draw attention to the nature of the connection between living and dead. Someone undertaking such a thing once he has gone through the gate of death is able to look at spiritual events the way a child looks at nature. The child looks at the natural world but does not understand it. But through an intuition he is able to convey marvellous things.

Things developed on the basis of intellectual thought will not reach the dead. The living individual must be available to the dead individual. The latter must be able to turn to the thoughts of the living, and what he experiences must be seen from the mirrors of the thoughts of the living within him.

Anthroposophy would never exist in the spiritual world if human beings had not gained it on earth. It is true, therefore, that initiates who work on earth have the thoughts in their souls by this roundabout route, and that the dead are able to take up these thoughts. One cannot say, why read to the dead, seeing that the dead live in the world about which we develop thoughts. Children also live in the world of which we speak. Children do not have the things that science provides on earth, but they are able to take in anthroposophy in the spiritual world. Yet this anthroposophy can only get to the dead from this earth.

I hope we understand one another in this. It is indeed evident that the individual who comes to you as one of the dead experiences something like a longing within him. He does not know, however, what this longing is aiming for. You meet with him, and if you are guided by entering into a relationship with him that is how you can work with the dead whatever the circumstances. If you have spiritual wisdom, it will be filled with light, and the dead perceive the light. But if the soul does not take in spiritual wisdom, it will stay dark and the dead cannot perceive it. The possibility for the dead to live with us depends on what we have to offer them.

That is the other side of what we were discussing this morning. We bring something about that gives the dead inner satisfaction, and it truly will be the best fruit of anthroposophical life and work that we do not merely believe in the life of the dead but that there will be more and more activity, activity in the soul, that will attract the dead. And this will be an increasing necessity for the development of our civilization. Human beings will be all the less connected with what remains to them of the life between death and rebirth the less they fill themselves with spiritual wisdom. In the physical world souls will have to grow more and more impoverished and cold unless they turn to the spiritual life. They gain inwardness only by communicating with the spiritual world.

One thought can live in our souls to strengthen them—our activity need not end when we have gone through the gate of death, nor need it end for the advance of civilization. No, we will be able to have an influence down below if people down there are prepared to receive it. If the spiritual world were open to us without the individual doing something for it, humanity would grow casual about it. No, we have to do something for it. This is indeed proof for us of the basic truth that flows to us from anthroposophy.

LECTURE 5

Today I intend to speak about an important concept in esoteric science. It concerns the connection between microcosm and macrocosm. In esoteric science we have a number of key terms, key themes that run through the whole esoteric movement. One is the concept of rhythmic number, another that of microcosm and macrocosm. The secret of number is evident in that certain phenomena follow one another so that the seventh occurrence may be said to mark the conclusion of an event, the eighth the beginning of a new event. In the physical world this fact is reflected in the relationship of the octave to the prime. For anyone seeking to enter into occult worlds, this principle becomes the basis for a comprehensive philosophy. Not only musical notes follow the law of number but also events in time. In the spiritual world events are arranged in such a way that we see a relationship there which is like that in the rhythm of musical notes.

The relationship between microcosm and macrocosm is even more important. We see it reflected wherever we go. Considering the way the whole plant relates to the seed, we see the whole plant to be a macrocosm, the seed a microcosm. In a way the forces distributed over the whole plant are brought together as if in a point in the seed. In a similar way we can call the development of an individual person from childhood to old age to be a microcosm, the development of a nation a macrocosm. Every nation has its childhood, when it takes in important elements of civilization. An example are the Romans who took in Greek civilization. A nation grows and develops and finds in itself the powers for further development. It is important, therefore, that the member of a nation goes through everything the nation goes through. He relates to his nation as the seed does to the plant. The highest degree of relation between microcosm and macrocosm we see in the human being, as he presents himself in the world perceived through the senses and the cosmos. The way a person is present in the world perceived through the senses is that the powers of the whole universe are concentrated in him or her, like the powers of the whole plant in the seed.

Now we may ask: Are these powers in the human being also spread out in some way in the macrocosm as the powers in the seed spread over the whole plant? The answer can only come from esoteric science, for in his life on earth the human being only gets to know himself as microcosm. Yet he does not only live in a microcosm, but has a life also in the universe.

Initially it is just words when we say that in their experience of the waking and the sleep state human beings alternate between life in the microcosm and life in the macrocosm. When we enter into sleep, the conscious mind ceases to be active, and effectively ceases to exist for us. An external science will fail in its attempts to find in a sleeping person the element that is his inner life when awake. Even just logically it is impossible to think that the inner life is destroyed on going to sleep and emerges again from the void on waking. In external science it will have to be admitted in the not too far distant future that external, material facts tell us as little of the inner life as knowing the laws pertaining to oxygen means we know the lung. We study the organic functions of the lung for this. And so we also realize that the external laws say nothing about the physical life which we inhale on waking and exhale on going to sleep. To the occultist, going to sleep and waking up is simply a breathing process. Where is this element of spirit and soul when the human being is asleep, corresponding to the air he has exhaled? Occult science shows that this element is enveloped by the spirit-world's atmosphere, just as we are enveloped by the airy atmosphere, the difference being that the latter extends for a few miles whilst the former fills the universe.

Let us consider the amount of air a human being has inhaled and relate this to the atmosphere as a whole—the air which has been inhaled into the human body becomes part of the atmosphere when exhaled. In occult terms we may thus say that after inhalation it is in the microcosm, after exhalation in the macrocosm. In the same way the life of soul and spirit which is active in our body is in the microcosm from waking to sleeping, in the macrocosm from going to sleep to waking. External physical science teaches existence of the physical atmosphere, occult science tells of the spiritual macrocosm that takes in our soul when we sleep.

Spiritual knowledge is gained by spiritual methods—by initiation. The life of the soul within the microcosm is known from daily experience, life within the macrocosm of spirit and soul becomes known to us through initiation. This science must be considered before the transition from microcosm to macrocosm can be understood. It gains particular significance because with it we enter into the spiritual world after death. Stepping on the threshold of death merely means that the soul is finally leaving the body. The method of initiation teaches subtle exercises for the soul. In everyday life we have an influence on our physical environment. We must get the soul into a condition where spirit and soul influence the macrocosm and gain impressions from it. We must seek to free our powers of spirit and soul which are bound to life in a body. Three powers of soul are bound up with the body in ordinary life, and initiation frees them. The first of these is the power of thought. In ordinary life we use it to form ideas, thoughts about the things around us. Let us try and enter into the nature of this power of thought. What happens when we think and form ideas? People who work in physical science will also admit that every time they have a thought relating to something perceived through the senses a process of destruction occurs in the brain. We have to destroy fine structures in the brain, as is sufficiently evident from the fact that we grow tired. Anything that has been destroyed by everyday thinking is restored again in sleep.

With the method of initiation we achieve a condition where we free the power of thought from the physical brain. In that case nothing is destroyed. We achieve this by means of meditation, concentration, contemplation. These are processes in the soul that differ from the ordinary inner life. The ideas and processes in the soul within us in everyday life are not really suitable for producing meditation in the soul.

Other processes have to be chosen for this. An example will show this. Imagine two glasses, one is empty, the other half full. Then imagine that we pour water from the half-filled glass into the empty one, and imagine that the half full one is getting fuller and fuller in the process. A materialist would consider this to be a foolish notion. But when we have an idea that is suitable for meditation it is not something real in the physical sense but something that creates ideas in the soul. It is exactly because it does not relate to anything real that this idea diverts the mind from reality. It can be a symbol, however, a symbol for the process in the soul that is bound up with the secret of love. Love is like the half-full glass. You pour some of its content into an empty glass and yet it gets fuller. The soul does not grow more empty; it grows fuller to the extent to which it gives away. Such can be the significance of this symbol.

If we now take such an idea and focus all the powers of our soul on it, that is meditation. We must forget all else, including ourselves. The whole of our inner life must be focused on it for a long time, something like a quarter of an hour. It is not enough to do such an exercise once or a few times; it has to be repeated over and over again. Depending on the individual's nature it will become evident that the inner life is changing in the process. We find that we develop a power of thought that does not destroy the brain. People going through this development will realize that the meditation does not tire them nor destroy the brain. The fact that beginners tend to go to sleep when meditating would seem to contradict this. But that is because we are still attached to the outside world in the beginning and have not yet freed our thoughts from the brain. When repeated efforts have freed the powers of thought from the brain, when we have learned to meditate without growing tired, the whole of our human life is transformed. We are now consciously the way we have until now been without conscious awareness and when out of the body during sleep. And just as we think our I within our skin in everyday life, so we experience ourselves out of the body after meditation. The body becomes an object for us to look at. But now we get to know this in a different way than we do in sleep. We get to know it like magnetic forces that chain us to the body. It is something we want to enter into wholly and completely. And we realize that the powers which draw us to our physical body every morning are the ones which before birth fetched us from the spiritual world, making us look for the hereditary streams to find a new body. This tells us why we felt drawn to our parents and ancestors.

There is one idea we can treat as an exception, an experience in the soul that differs from those we have at the transition from microcosm to macrocosm. Looking at the body from the macrocosm we say with everything we learn: 'This is outside of us.' Once we have woken the Paul experience[22] in us, however, we have developed a soul element that is even then an outer one in us. When we are out of the body we feel the Christ experience to be an inner one. We may call this the first meeting with the Christ impulse in the macrocosm.

We must now consider a second kind of initiation power. Just as we free the power of thought so we can also release the power which we use to express ourselves in speech. In materialistic science the view is that motor speech organs have their centre in Broca's area in the brain.[23] But it is not that Broca's area has developed speech but rather that speech has developed Broca's area.

The power of thought is destructive; speech, coming from the social environment, is constructive. We are now able to release the power which Broca's area develops. We do so by imbuing our meditation with feeling values. When I meditate on 'Wisdom shines in the light', this again does not reflect an external truth, but it does have profound meaning. If we imbue our feelings with 'We want to live with all the light that lets wisdom shine' we feel how we take hold of the power which otherwise comes to expression in words and now lives in our soul. When we speak of silence being golden this refers to the following. We have a power in our soul which creates the word. We can take hold of this just as we do of the power of thought. We then overcome time, just as by taking hold of the power of thought we overcome space. Memory which in everyday life goes back to childhood will then extend to life before birth. This is the way of learning about the life from our last death to our present birth, and also the way of seeing through human evolution. We see through the powers that guide the evolution of human history.

And we gain insight into the life from birth to death. When we develop the power of the unspoken word we gain insight into the spiritual basis of life on earth. Here we come again to a historical event, the Mystery on Golgotha. For this is the road along which we find the ascending and descending evolution of humanity and the point where the Christ incarnated. He is recognized the way he is in his very own power. By freeing thought we connect with the Christ as he was on earth. By freeing the word we connect with the Mystery on Golgotha. This casts a special light on the first line in John's Gospel.

A third power also gains independence through meditation. It involves not only brain and larynx but also the circulation and the heart. We are aware of it in a low-level activity when we blush or grow pale. There a soul element intervenes in the blood's pulsation, going as far as the heart. This power of the soul may be withdrawn from the blood's pulsation and become an independent inner power. It comes about through meditation at the point where the will enters into it. We meditate 'Wisdom shines in the light' but decide to connect our will to act with it in such a way that we want to go with this radiant wisdom in human evolution. When we come to such a will meditation we get the powers of will to flow into the soul. We can find these powers and withdraw them from the blood—though not entirely—and they then create a power of clairvoyance which allows us to go beyond our earth. We come to perceive the earth to be a re-embodied planet that will re-embody again and we human beings with it. Thus we grow into the macrocosm through the world of spirit and soul. In a way we learn how life between death and birth must be the opposite of life in an incarnation. An initiate learns about experiences gained after death, free of the body. Let us take the main characteristic of what has been offered to us when free of the body. It is the same experience as in life after death. Living in the microcosm we gain perceptions through the physical organ of the senses. After death we look at the body as the initiate does. Then we cannot perceive the things which our sense organs perceive. The initiate is able to recognize the life between death and rebirth because he has made the transition from microcosm to macrocosm whilst still here.

We cannot converse with the dead in ordinary human language. But when we have freed the power of speech we can see how we are together with the dead. By freeing the power of thought we are able to converse with those who are between death and rebirth.

Let me give you an example. A seer was able to converse with a dead individual who had been a splendid person but had cared for his family only in material terms. He had no religious and anthroposophical ideas. The seer was able to learn the following from this individual: 'I know I have lived with my family and they were my sunshine. They are still alive, I know, but I am only able to see them up to the point in time where I left the earth. It is not possible to make a connection with them.' Conditions are complicated after death. The seer was able to see that the wife still showed something in her nature of the consequences of having been with her husband. The husband was able to see these consequences but not the way we see a person but as if in a mirror. There is a way of seeing when over there, but it is as if it were a mirror image. This feels hideous because one does not see the real person, as he or she is. In the world perceived through the senses we see the bodily aspect; afterwards we must be able to see the soul aspect. But just as we do not see a candle in a dark room unless it has been lit, so in this case, too, insight is reduced, dimmed down. It is nevertheless possible for the dead individual and the individual on earth to be connected if the latter imbues himself with spiritual life. That is the basis for the good we can do for the dead. Someone has gone through the gate of death with whom we share certain interests—we can read to him. We imagine that he is there before us and read to him in silence; we can also send him thoughts. But we will only gain an impression if we send him ideas and concepts that have spiritual life. The mission of anthroposophy will be understood if we know that we must get rid of the abyss that separates us from the dead.

Souls that had been opposing anthroposophy may also feel that being thus read to is a benison. There are two sides to our inner life—consciously living through things and the deep down parts of the soul which like the depths of the sea are evident only in the waves at the top. We may hear, for instance, that only one of two brothers is an anthroposophist whilst the other opposes anthroposophy. This can only be a fact in the outside world. The inner process is that there is a profound longing for something religious and one seeks to numb this by rejecting anthroposophy. The idea one has in one's conscious mind is merely an opiate so that one may forget what is there in the depths. Death removes all this and then we do indeed hunger for what we had unconsciously longed for. This is why reading anthroposophical writings to them is such a benison. Awareness of being connected with the dead comes gradually. But even before that we risk nothing more than that the dead individual does not listen when we read to him. We see, therefore, that the dead and the living, microcosm and macrocosm, connect with one another when anthroposophical teaching is taken up in a living way.

This also happens in another sphere. When the seer observes people who are asleep, he sees that souls go through the gate of sleep that never have any spiritual interests and others that take in spiritual thoughts during the day. A difference is apparent. The sleeping souls are like seed grain in a field. There would be starvation in the spiritual world if no spiritual thoughts were brought there. The dead feed on the spiritual, the anthroposophical ideas brought there by people going to sleep. If we do not take spiritual concepts with us on going to sleep, we deprive the dead of food. By reading to them we give them spiritual stimulus; the spiritual ideas we take with us on going to sleep nourish the dead.

Human beings become a bridge between microcosm and macrocosm by being active in their souls. The things we make our own are like a seed grain. I would say the living and not just the theoretical mission of anthroposophy is as follows. Theory is transformed into the elixir of life, immortality is experienced. Just as a seed guarantees the next seed, so do we develop powers in spirit and soul that guarantee a coming back in a next life on earth. We do not merely understand, but live the immortality in us. That is how we experience that which goes through the gate of death from the moment when our hair goes grey. In this sense anthroposophy will be the elixir of life, like the blood that moves through our physical body. And only then will anthroposophy be what it is meant to be. If we come to realize this and want to sum it up in a fundamental feeling, the fundamental feeling that the human soul is connected with the spiritual world as our physical body is connected with the physical world, human beings will know that,

They speak to the human mind,
The spirits in the far horizons of space,
They change as time progresses.
In living experience the human soul,
Not limited by horizons of space
Nor lost in the progress of time,
Enters the realm of the eternities.

LECTURE 6

STOCKHOLM, 8 JUNE 1913

THE first of the subjects chosen for this brief course of lectures is about 'nature and spirit in the light of spiritual-scientific insight'. Nature and spirit! That seems to be a contradiction which will immediately bring to mind all kinds of opposing views and opinions that have been put forward in the world. We know, don't we, that a kind of science has progressively evolved in recent centuries where only nature is said to count, and the point of view is that it is really hardly possible to include the spirit. On the other hand we see how defenders of the spirit and of spiritual life do make themselves heard in all fields even today. And we need only look to the utmost extreme on one side where people said in the nineteenth century: 'The brain secretes thoughts the way the liver secretes bile.'[24] 'Anything by way of spirit we perceive in human beings is therefore a purely natural process, and we do not believe in any other kind of spirit.' All we have to do is to put this side by side with the many current endeavours to establish a science of the spirit and we have the two extremes.

It is, however, also possible to think differently about the words 'nature' and 'spirit' and refer to Goethe's words: 'Nature is sin, the intellect's ideas are Satan's, and between them Doubt is bred, the mongrel offspring of their monstrous bed.'[25] We can thus think of many things that put nature and spirit in opposition, many things that have brought disharmony to human hearts, provoking tempests of battle and strife in the world.

On the other hand there are the words from more recent times, also from Goethe, that the spirit never exists and is active without matter, nor matter without spirit. This is very easy to refute. We merely have to draw attention to the fact that I need only chip a piece of granite from a rock and I have matter without spirit.[26] Refutations of profound words are easily found in the world, and we must clearly understand, especially in a spiritual-scientific movement, that nothing is easier for the foolish element in the world but to refute the words of the wise, seemingly with the greatest justification. For an anthroposophical view we must go more deeply into these things.

What is spirit and what is nature? In the ordinary way we are in no doubt about it that we encounter nature when we see the plants sprouting from the ground in spring, when we see them unfold. There we see nature alive and active. Nor is there any doubt that we speak of nature with some justification when snowflakes cover the ground in winter. Both of these things are happening in nature. But have we been involved in what goes on around us with full justification? Just imagine creatures that are much, much smaller than we are, so small that our nails or hair would be as large to them as trees are to us. And imagine that they are able to think. They would describe the hair on our head the way we describe plants rising from the ground. We human beings do not describe single hairs nor the human head as a soil from which the individual hairs rise, for we know that we cannot find a hair in nature that is an entity in itself. You would need to be so small that you could not take in the hairs as a whole for you to describe a hair by itself. Such a creature might perhaps be able to distinguish individual hairs. It might arrange them in classes and orders according to the site where they grow—a class of left temple hairs, a class of right temple hairs; a class of left forehead hairs, a class of right forehead hairs; they might later give them names to distinguish them further. So there might be a hair science for such small creatures. There is such a science, with some justification, for other entities—botany. The earth seen as a whole does indeed bring forth individual plants just as our head produces hair. Individual plants belong to the earth and are not a particular genus, but in botany they are classified and described without considering that this plant world is a single whole that belongs to the earth, just as our hairs are a single whole with our organism. Nature or the world do not care in the least if people create a botany for themselves, just as people would not care if a tiny thinking creature were to create its own hair science.

Spiritual science does, however, take us even further. It shows that just as you cannot think of a creature such as a human being with hairs on his head without a soul, so you cannot consider the earth in any other way but as a whole that has all material, natural things as organs of the earth spirit or the earth soul. Further study of this earth spirit or this earth soul shows in the first place that it differs from the human soul. It is peculiar to the human soul that it presents itself to us as a kind of single whole. It is not like this with the earth spirit to begin with. Ultimately there is a governing earth spirit, as you know, but the next thing we find in our spiritual study of the earth is a great sum total, an abundance, of elemental spirits; in great numbers and of many kinds they are the next level of the earth spirit.

We may first of all consider this earth spirit. We find that in the hemisphere where it happens to be summer at a particular time, for instance, these elementals of the earth spirit go through a kind of sleep, and they are awake there when it is winter. Spiritual insight actually shows that elemental spirits go to sleep to the same degree as plants rise from the ground. In winter there is a stirring; the elemental spirits then form ideas, have sentience and feelings in their own way. For the earth, the night of human beings is summer in the hemisphere where it happens to be summer, and the day of human beings is winter. The earth as a whole wakes and sleeps like a human being, but in such a way that one half is always more awake, the other more asleep; human beings, on the other hand, are organized in such a way that they sleep altogether all at once. That, too, is not quite correct, for it is exactly for human beings the way it is for the earth. When a human being sleeps it is only the head part which is sleeping, with the other organs all the more awake. But human beings are not made to be aware of this. It is really also the same with the earth, though not entirely so. One hemisphere has more water than the other, and because of this, sleeping and waking is not so different for earth from the sleeping and waking of human beings.

We consider human beings to have life and a soul, and we have to do the same with the earth. It is just because we are small creatures relative to the earth that we do not see that it also has life and a soul. But that is also due to our materialistic age. Kepler,[27] for example, who certainly also knew how to think, did still say that he saw the earth as a large organism. He did not have an occult view of the earth and so he did not know that winter means waking and summer sleeping for the earth. He imagined the earth to be like a huge whale rather than thinking of it as an ensouled creature at a higher level than a human being. He reduced the situation a little, seeing the earth as a whale, and he considered the movement of the air to be the creature's breathing in and out. Giordano Bruno[28] held the same view. To him, the earth was a huge ensouled organism, with ebb and flood its breathing. And Goethe, too, saw the earth as a huge living individual that showed its breathing in and out process in air currents and in the oceans. Yes, people of that earlier, more spiritual time did still know that we cannot look at the earth in the abstract, theoretical way in which people do today, as if one could describe a hair or a nail on its own, whereas one should know that these cannot exist without the whole organism, that they have their source and origin in the whole organism. The naturalistic way of looking at this does not get the point. In looking at the world it is important and with everything in the world we must be able to ask ourselves: 'Is that part of a whole or it is a whole in itself?' If you find a human tooth you must not see it as a single creature, for the tooth only has a real basis if seen as part of the human being. And it is equally absurd to describe a single plant, for it can only be envisaged as a part of the whole earth. And the outer body of the earth can only be envisaged with the earth's soul and spirit. And if one doesn't know about the spirit of the earth, if one does not know that this earth is the body of a spirit, in the same way as our own body, then one does, of course, look at the earth in the way it is done in mineralogy, geology, botany. There is no awareness behind this that behind everything that is described is the governing spirit of the earth. It is easy to say when I break a piece off a rock that there is no spirit in it. There is no spirit in a piece of tooth, but that piece of tooth cannot be envisaged without the whole human being and the soul and spirit to which it belongs.

We have to keep this in mind when we speak of nature and spirit. If we therefore talk about the earth as a natural planet and do not refer to its soul and spirit, this is merely because we are ignoring the spirit, don't want to know about it. Where does the earth exist as a mere natural planet? In botany, geology, astronomy people would say that it moves in cosmic space. If that were true it would soon stop moving, it would break down the way the human body does after death when the spirit has departed.

This way of looking at the world has spread. Even human limbs and the whole human being are today described as if they were sheer nature, which means that people are looking at the corpse. For if human beings were the way they are described in physiology, anatomy and so on, they would have to die on the spot. In physiology one gets sheer fantasy, the same in astronomy, and also in geology with its description of the earth. This is nothing but fantasy. There is no such thing as this purely natural earth. For the fact that the earth is the way it is has its basis, down to the smallest piece of rock, in that the earth is filled with the earth spirit.

There we see what really matters. In looking at the human being it is important to find the starting point, going from the part to the whole, and that we do not remove little bits of the whole. The human being as such is a whole. And when we come to the earth, we must consider all of it to be a whole. If we separate nature and its influences from the earth, what then is this nature? It is then the product of our fantasies which actually does not exist at all but merely presents itself to us as if it were because we are cutting a part off the whole. So we see that it is not a question of describing something most faithfully but of knowing how a part fits into the whole or rather grows from the whole. That is how the earth must be regarded, as a whole, not a physical whole but an entity with a body, an entity that belongs to its spirit.

We might also speak of nature and spirit in another way. All we need to do is look at the human being as such. In a way we have something there which appears to justify the terms 'nature' and 'spirit' as opposites. A child is born, and all signs of life in the early days appear to be something developed out of the physical, out of the infant's whole physical nature. Because of this people often say that the child was still acting wholly out of his nature and that the spiritual aspect and the soul would only be born from the body later on. At the beginning of life the human being is more nature, they say, later he develops more the spirit. But once again this is nothing but a careless way of looking at things. For there is much spirit in us in the early part of life; it is only that it is there in a much more hidden way than later. Everything that gives the body its forms is active spirit, but it is not the case that we are inwardly active in the spirit and let our powers of memory throw light on it. We truly do not have less spirit in us in the early years of childhood than we do in later years. One might perhaps put it in an even more radical way. Someone asked me the other day: What does it mean when a child lives for just a few days and then dies? Occult science shows that such a short life does nevertheless have meaning. It is often the case that the spirit which is in this body has been able to develop much, but perhaps there is one thing it has not been able to develop, a really sound way of seeing, for example. Let us assume someone has been an excellent person in one incarnation but did have poor eyesight. It will happen then, that such an individual lives for just a few days in a later incarnation, merely to make up for what was missing in the previous life because of those weak eyes. In this case we have to add this incarnation to the previous one. People generally very much underestimate the significance of a child's learning powers in those first days. It needs a greater capacity for a child to look into the light than it does for everything you learn in your first term at university.

All kinds of objections may be raised here, but if you just think about the subject you will no doubt see that it is correct. We only see childhood in the right way when we know that at that time the spirit is just as much in the body as we develop the brain, our physiognomy and so on as it is later on when we are being astute. At a later age the spirit will have withdrawn a bit more from the body and acts as the more abstract mind and spirit which is then no longer able, however, to organize the brain. That will have solidified by then. The principle people really like to call 'spirit' later on in life did already exist in the first part of human life but had something else to do then, being more connected with the forces of nature. We just do not see it and we therefore say that what is happening there is nature only, and what happens consciously later on is spirit only. This is why people assume 'natural' processes in early childhood and the spiritual nature of our thinking, feeling and doing* in later life to be opposites. But the polar opposition lies elsewhere.

In infancy nature and spirit are closely connected, they interpenetrate, are still friends. Later they go apart, and the spirit and the natural processes proceed more separately. This means that the natural processes are more spiritless, the spirit having been differentiated out from them to be the separate soul of which human beings are so proud. The price we have to pay for this is that the body is more spiritless. Initially the human being drew spirit from the body so that he might use it more separately for himself. Similar things happened through Earth evolution. In very early earth times the spirit was closely bound up with earth nature, and so earth spirit and earth nature worked closely together. Today earth nature has been as much separated from its spirit as nature is from the soul element in human beings. And just as in the human being it is the spirit which governs thinking, feeling and doing, so does the earth spirit, as a course of history, run side by side with the natural process in Earth evolution. In the Lemurian age[29] these were still more closely connected, just as spiritual and nature processes are still more closely allied in infants compared to people in later life. What really matters here? Is it a matter of saying 'The spirit develops later in life or in Earth's evolution?' No, it was there to begin with, but at the time it directed its activities towards the part that was then separated off. And that hardens, grows woody and dies off.

Because of this we must also consider a whole that we want to consider not just at a time nor in its parts. As a child the human being is not a physical whole on earth. The human being in youth, middle age, old age, and so on is a whole and we cannot say that he develops from being natural to being spiritual. No, we must say that in early childhood nature and spirit were closely bound up with one another in the human being. Later they grew more separate. This makes the natural principle a bit more dead, a bit less inwardly alive, and the spirit grows more independent. So there has been a process of differentiation in the human being as a whole. That is the right idea. But it is not the case that the spiritual simply develops from the natural. Differentiation occurs.

---

* Alternative translation: thinking, feeling and will.

When we speak of nature without the spirit we are talking of a mere figment of our imagination. Under present physical conditions on earth no human being could develop into the creature able to think, feel and will who is so proud of his or her mental and spiritual capacities unless he or she had first separated mind and spirit from natural existence. We have to learn to think in a completely new way about nature and spirit.

There is more to come. Let us consider the outward nature of man and woman. If this is done very superficially the conclusion will be that the woman is closer to nature, forming opinions more directly on the basis of nature, whereas the man has moved away more from nature. Independent thinking lives in him, more of an independent mind and spirit. The materialistic age, where the mind and spirit is seen in a materialistic way, has yielded further reasons for the difference, for instance the weight of the brain. However, when they weighed the brain of the individual who had produced this theory they found that he had a specially small male brain! So if we consider nature and spirit in this way, even a superficial glance will show that this is not the case. The outward appearance of a woman is, however, more natural in some respect for, in her, activity of mind and spirit has not yet separated so much from the bodily principle as is the case with a man. Women are more natural on the present-day earth because in them activity of mind and spirit has not yet separated as much from the bodily principle as is the case with men. We should not think of men having greater spirituality than women; it is merely that distilled spirit, which leaves matter aside, is more in evidence. The female body is more filled with spirit, like that of the child, for instance; the male body has less spirit in it at a later age than it does in youth. We should not, however, speak of male nature or female nature being more natural or more spiritual.

Our way of looking at things must change, therefore. It is true to say that in some respect the principle connected with male and female nature stays with us through life. It is not always easy to have to refer to this. Why, for example, are there more women than men in the Anthroposophical Society? Surely this suggests a lack of intellect in anthroposophy? It is fairly easy to give an objective answer to this, but one may easily be misunderstood. The fact that more women come to the Anthroposophical Society, that is, that they find it easier to make spiritual truths their own, exists because they retain more of the spirituality of nervous system and brain. In men this separates earlier from the bodily principle, and so they do not find it so easy to take in the element which speaks to something in them which is neither male nor female but is above them—the human essence as such.

In a single incarnation people are either male or female. In a man the hardened parts are more developed, and the spirit—the temporal, transitory spirit—is a bit more distilled out from his general nature. In women, nature and spirit continue to be more connected throughout life, and this makes them more flexible by nature. But the spiritual truths address themselves to something in the human being that has nothing to do with the difference between male and female. For the essence, the entity that moves from one incarnation to another, may be alternating between male and female, albeit men are not always too happy about this.

The deepest essence of ourselves has nothing to do with male and female. In the same way the deepest essence of the phenomena and facts of the world has absolutely nothing to do with nature and spirit, for it will take a more spiritual form on one occasion and a more natural one on another. Both are phases in one existence, and life does progress. In human life, activities more of soul and spirit during the day alternate with activities which are more natural for the physical human being during the night. In the universe, spirits have times when they are more spiritual by nature and other times when they grow more 'natural'. This is a rhythm in the universe. Looking at the essential nature of a person, for instance, when he is a man in an incarnation and thus karmically condemned to distil the spirit from the natural, he can say to himself: 'At present I am karmically destined to distil the spirit from nature, but this must alternate rhythmically, in a cycle, with being a woman, when I'll be allowed to be more in the natural aspect with my spirit. So I will be granted a pendulum swing towards natural existence again.'

This is how it is with all planets, all wholes, totalities, with all worlds. Where we find something natural there will be something spiritual that belongs to it, and where we find a spiritual principle, it will have the tendency to separate something off from itself which will be natural.

Nature and spirit are not opposites but alternating states of a higher principle which is behind them.

We have to see, therefore, that when we take the spiritual point of view many an older term that has been dreadfully misused needs to be corrected. Once we no longer describe mere parts of something which is really a whole we will also get a clear understanding of the terms spirit and nature, no longer limiting ourselves by taking a one-sided view. We will realize then that the spirit would be something very weak if nature were inimical to it; we shall realize that nature is something which the spirit puts outside of it for a time, like a snail secreting its shell. But the spirit is also able to take nature back into itself and dissolve it in itself again. It then makes it invisible but has it inside itself, having become a single whole again. If perfect oneness of spirit and nature did exist anywhere this would mean that where facts are concerned the spirit has dissolved all the nature that belongs to it.

Let us assume someone is 40 years old. He has his essential nature and he has his soul, his spirit, of which he is so proud. If we go back to his childhood it is more a whole, but this means that it presents more in its natural basis. If we go even further back, to before his birth, he'll be all spirit; he then still had all spirituality without natural basis, without matter, in him.

It is a pendulum swing in the world. The essence creates its image in the natural aspect, revealing itself through this. The spirit bears nature within it in order to create an image with the element to which it gives birth within it. But the essence also has the power to take up everything that exists out there in nature into the spirit. And so the spirit can overcome all the images of itself, to appear evermore in new transformations, new configurations. This tells us that infinitely many configurations rest within the essence, and that the meaning of the world truly lies in there being ever new developments. If we are able to see that spirit and nature belong together, cannot be separated, we come to what really matters in the world.

LECTURE 7

As you devote yourself to spiritual life it will be necessary to be aware as to why we the people of the present age, taking up our mission as people of the present age, have the longing and urge to cultivate spiritual life. The reason is that from the end of the last century people can relate in a completely different way to the higher worlds than was the case in earlier centuries. This is not fully taken into account, that from age to age human evolution yields ever new impulses.

In the fourteenth, fifteenth and sixteenth centuries it was relatively difficult for human souls to develop understanding for the spiritual world, for spiritual life. In the times ahead it will be more and more of a natural need in the human soul to seek spiritual insight. For in a sense the gates to the spiritual world have been open from the last third of the nineteenth century onwards, so that spiritual insight flows from the spiritual world for all who wish to receive it. In this sense we are in a completely new phase in human evolution. People who are today drawn to anthroposophy, to the anthroposophical movement, as though by an instinct simply have a feeling for the signs of the times. Fifty years ago it would have been completely impossible for people to meet the way we are doing today to talk about spiritual secrets of existence. At that time the waves of spiritual insight did not yet flow down to humanity. We have to understand that our aims and intentions in this respect are something that must grow more and more general. For this, we must for once look for the symptoms that characterize the whole present-day development of humanity. At present only a few people are interested in spiritual life and feel the urge to gain insight into the spiritual world. The masses are still vigorously rejecting any spiritual insight. We must know how to enter deeply into the causes of this situation in human evolution. Most important among the current ideas which show what has become symptomatic of the present age is perhaps the idea of freedom. It is the idea which can best illustrate for us the evolution over recent centuries.

It is perfectly natural for people in the world today who are not seeking spiritual insight but who do want to be informed about the laws that govern the world and the inner life of human beings to resort to official information which in turn is governed by natural science. For how do people gain insight into the world? They turn to others who have learned to gain natural-scientific understanding of the world and have perhaps also produced popular science writings about how one should think about the human soul, about nature and freedom, and so on. How could anyone arrive at any idea other than that you have to turn to those people?

Official knowledge did, however, go through a very strange development in the nineteenth century at the point where it sought to be a philosophy of life, and this is symptomatic. People completely fail to take note exactly of such extremely strange symptoms. If you ask one of the great men or women of science if there is such a thing as an idea of freedom, the answer will be: 'It does not exist in the sense in which the idea was seen in the old philosophies of life, for we know today that when someone ingests some particular substance or another, for instance, this will immediately affect the brain, and he will then no longer be able to use his brain in the right way. One sees that human beings are dependent on their brains, so how can they be free?' Or it will be: 'In rationalistic psychology we show that someone who is suffering from a mental illness and is unable to talk, or cannot recall speech sounds, shows abnormalities in the brain. So how can one speak of freedom when human beings are dependent on their brains?' That is what people say in ordinary psychiatry. All these reasons carry a lot of weight in people's everyday thinking. They sound very plausible and gradually settle in people's minds and unless a spiritual philosophy of life puts their heads in order again people will have a philosophy of life where the idea of freedom is wholly denied.

Science has followed a strange course in this respect. In the eighteenth and early nineteenth centuries people were always looking for design and purpose in the natural world. They would ask themselves: 'Why does the bull have horns, why do apples grow on apple trees?' The conclusion was that a wise providence had done this. It gave horns to the bull so that it might thrust, and let apples grow so that people might eat them, and so on. Enlightened minds of the eighteenth and nineteenth centuries made a lot of fun of those ideas about usefulness. Ironically they'd say: 'Why has world existence let this tree grow or that one? Because people like to drink wine and need corks for their wine bottles.'

Such objections to an anthropomorphic view of nature are perfectly justifiable. With a person we can always ask what their design and purpose is in doing the things they do. So nature had been made anthropomorphic, and an anthropomorphic view was taken of the world, asking after nature's aims just as one asks about people's aims. It was perfectly justifiable for people of the nineteenth century to object to an anthropomorphism where people did not see anything in nature as such but had superimposed the human being on nature. Nineteenth-century people wanted to study nature directly, asking nature herself. They did not want to impose design and purpose, the purpose known to man, on nature. And they were right in this, for the old way of looking at things applied human soul life to nature. And it is justifiable to say that one wants to study nature the way it is, separate from the human being. People said: 'We want to cast out from nature everything that belongs to man.' This led to an image of nature in the nineteenth century that had nothing in it of the human being. A materialistic science of nature developed. Human concepts were removed from nature. In a sense it was the right kind of reaction to the old idea of usefulness, to teleology.

A materialistic natural science thus arose, with the premise that nothing of the human being be found in it. At the time it was perfectly justifiable. But in the second half of the nineteenth century the idea came that the human being must be seen in the same way as nature is seen. This second demand, to consider the human being according to the material situation in the natural world, changed things completely, for the human being had been taken out of the natural world. It was perfectly clear then that the human being simply could not be found in a natural science of that kind. This evolved in the course of the nineteenth century. Everything belonging to the human soul had been distilled out of natural science and this was much the same as saying: 'I have here a bottle with water in it. But I want to have an empty bottle and therefore pour the water away.' And one is then surprised that there is no more water in the bottle. Everyone then notices immediately that the bottle is empty. With natural science, people did not realize how foolish it is to want to understand the human being by means of a nature from which the human being had been removed. I am convinced that a gathering of materialists would merely laugh about this simple way of looking at it, for people are not aware of this major error. It was the idea of freedom, of immortality and the like which had to suffer most due to this misconception. For anyone who looks at it the way I have just described would find it perfectly natural and one cannot gain enlightenment concerning these terms from natural science.

For a spiritual philosophy of life it is particularly important to win through to the realization that in their bodily nature human beings do indeed belong to the natural world outside and its laws, but that they bear something in them as their soul which can only be found by using the spiritual approach. In other words, if we want to perceive the human being in his very own essential nature we must not look at the outward form human beings have between birth and death but at the principle which continues from incarnation to incarnation and is his true essential nature. It will be the mission of anthroposophy to direct people's attention to aspects of inner life that prove to them that within the human being there is such an eternal core and essence which is independent of his bodily nature.

If we admit, as we begin to consider the human being, that his essential nature lives not only between birth and death but that it is something which places the human being in physical existence and also continues after death, we will see that it is necessary to take human knowledge and insight up into the regions where the essential human being has a part, thanks to his insight, in the higher world to which he belongs by being endowed with soul and spirit. But the moment human beings enter into the higher worlds with their insight they meet there with the spirits of those higher worlds just as here in the physical world they meet with the entities belonging to the three realms of nature.

The most unjustifiable view was expressed on one occasion by Pascal,[30] for instance, the well-known Christian philosopher, and has today been reaffirmed by Maeterlinck,[31] for example, saying that Pascal did want this once and for all. Pascal said that all that earthy existence really does for us is to hide eternity, infinity, from us.[32] One has to say that this is a widely accepted belief. Listen all around and you will everywhere find a justifiable longing for the spiritual, the eternal, and this is expressed by saying: 'Earthly existence is not at all satisfactory. Human beings truly gain real satisfaction only when they behold the eternal.' Yet when one truly penetrates to the eternal worlds something will be added to Pascal's words. For when you penetrate to eternity you will find that it does not in the least hide earthly existence but rather that it shows one that everything in that other world is designed to guide us once again to a further earthly existence.

People often have the oddest objections to the theory of reincarnation. When I had given a lady all the reasons why reincarnation is necessary she said: 'I don't want to return to earth, I don't like the life very much.' I tried to explain that her feelings were beside the point. She listened to what I had to say and then went home. She sent me a picture postcard from the next railway station. It said: 'I just don't want to be born again.' We may laugh about such an attitude, but it is quite common. People don't realize that their attitude to this does not matter, nor does anything they said here on earth during the present life. They don't know that it may be quite immaterial if one wants to come back or not. They don't know that between death and rebirth one has all the powers in one's soul that seek reincarnation and want to come back. These powers are indeed there. Over there everything is organized so that the powers which one develops there may be satisfied as one enters into life on earth again. One has a feeling that the soul did not achieve perfection, that it did not develop certain qualities in the last life on earth. Here on earth it may be all the same for one if one is perfect or not, but that is not so in the life between death and rebirth. There irresistible forces compel one to transform imperfection into perfection. One realizes that in many cases this can only be achieved at the cost of pain and suffering, and one knows that to achieve perfection one must accept the pain and pleasures of a life on earth. And one then goes full steam into a new incarnation.

I have told you this because such a thing makes us see very clearly that our philosophy of life must cover all angles and we must not draw conclusions as to the desires and interests one will have between death and rebirth from the way life between birth and death appears to us in our desires and interests. People will only learn to think in a thorough, energetic way when they use the spiritual philosophy of life and train themselves to be all-rounders in this way, when they come to realize that everything needs to be considered from different angles. Practical life does already force us to do so day by day. People are quite right when they say that fire is a great boon. Yet it is also true to say that fire causes great harm, burning down towns and villages. It is not possible to be absolute and say 'Fire is good', or 'Fire is an evil'. When it comes to fire, practical life teaches us to accept that there are two sides to it. Yet when we are asked to do the same with spirits of the higher worlds, Lucifer and Ahriman, for instance, we are reluctant to accept this. Instead we tend to ask: 'Is Lucifer a good or an evil spirit?' and 'Is Ahriman a good or an evil spirit?' People want to have definitions to answer those questions, and an answer like 'Lucifer and Ahriman may be both good and evil' is considered unsatisfactory. There is no such demand when it comes to fire. There everyday life makes us change a wrong opinion into a right one.

One of the many things currently circulating in Germany to attack us is that it was recently said, 'In his public lectures he [meaning Dr Steiner] presents things the way they appear from his point of view, but avoids giving definite ideas or opinions.' Well, my friends, in a Greek school of philosophy they once sought to gain a definite idea of what a human being is. Following long discussions it was agreed to say that a human being walks on two legs and does not have feathers. The next day someone brought along a plucked chicken and said, 'This, then, is a human being, for it has two legs and no feathers. According to our definition it ought to be a human being.' The problem with 'definite ideas' is that when one looks more closely they may prove to be very far from reality. Because of this, the spiritual view of life will particularly get people in the habit of considering things from all angles. A good bit of one-sided thinking has been produced in natural science, and even people of good will who seek to rise a bit above natural-scientific thinking often show a naivety worthy of our admiration. This is a field where one must gradually develop the will to be really clear about things.

Yesterday[33] I tried to show how people whom we may call thorough natural scientists and whose reputations shall not be blackened are unable to form an opinion particularly in the field of spiritual-scientific investigation. In the same way we must not let ourselves be taken aback by an idea which is no doubt presented with the best intentions but nevertheless won't stand up to scrutiny. An example would be the chemist and physicist William Crookes.[34] He achieved significant things in scientific research and at the same time was fully committed to the study of immortality. He wanted to know of immortality for certain, using normal scientific methods, and achieved excellent results in his work with mediums.[35] On one occasion he put forward an idea in such a way that up to a point one could go along with it. When someone says that our ability to see colours depends on the nature of our eyes, and the ability to hear sounds on our ears, and if we had different sense organs the world around us would look very different that is absolutely correct. And when he says, 'Why do you deny the existence of a supersensible world which also does not exist for you because you do not have the organs to perceive it?' that, too, is correct. He defined this idea more clearly, saying: 'We perceive colours, we hear sounds, but in the case of electricity and magnetism we only see the effects. These are natural forces the nature of which is not known to us though we do make use of them in everyday life.' It is something we find everywhere that people say these are natural forces which human beings have not fathomed. True enough. In reality all this means is that people have their eyes for colour, their ears for sound, and so on; in the case of magnetism they do see that a magnet attracts iron, but they do not see magnetism itself, the actual nature of it. In the case of electricity they perceive light and heat produced by it but not the electricity itself. William Crookes says: 'What would the world look like for someone endowed with special sense organs that allow them to perceive electricity and magnetism as such but unable to perceive light, colours, sounds, and so on? If we were unable to perceive light, a crystal would be opaque to us, for example, and so would glass, and there would be no point in having windows. They would merely prevent us from relating to the outside world. If on the other hand we had organs for electric currents, a telegraph wire would appear as a line of light passing through the darkness; we would perceive the flow and light of electricity. With an organ for magnetism we would be able to perceive magnets letting magnetic forces radiate out in all directions, and so on.' He also says: 'It is not beyond the bounds of possibility that there are entities with organs set for wavelengths that leave our organs untouched. Such entities live in a world different from our own.' He then goes on to consider what this world would look like. Glass and crystal would be dark bodies in this world, metals a bit brighter because they conduct electricity, with dark parts interspersed. A telegraph wire would be a long, narrow hole in a body of impenetrable solidity. A functioning dynamo would be similar to a major fire, and a magnet would actually fulfil the dream of medieval mystics of an eternal lamp that would never go out.

William Crookes has explained it all very well, and the method serves to give people a notion of how senseless it is to say that this physical world perceived through the senses is the only one, that there is no other world apart from our own, and that there can be no other entities but human beings. All of it true! But we can also say something else about this idea—and this is where the other side of the matter begins, the one that concerns the true spiritual scientist. Let us consider asking the question 'What would it be like if instead of eyes people really had these organs for direct perception of electricity and magnetism, if this idea put forward naively by someone were to be brought to realization for us human beings?' We would then find our way about in the realm of electricity and magnetism but not in the realm of light and sound. But there would be a consequence. If people had an organ for the direct perception of electricity and magnetism they would have not only this organ, which would be an organ of perception, but also the power to kill any other person or make them sick. Such an organ would directly confer that power.

So this is what can be said about William Crookes's idea from the point of view of spiritual science, for we know that forces related to magnetic and electrical forces are present in human beings here on earth. The question now has a very different meaning, and we really see the naivety of simply setting up such an idea. Someone who does not possess higher vision sets up the idea of looking into electrical and magnetic forces, but for the spiritual scientist this leads directly to what has just been said. If we bring that to mind we begin to see clearly that we must not stay on the surface but truly seek to go deeply into the wisdom that lies behind the world order and understand it. For the spiritual scientist's insight shows that it is a very good thing for human beings not to have the electrical and magnetic organs, for in this way they will not be able to damage others with them. Their lower instincts and desires thus also cannot run free initially, causing disaster to them and to others. Human beings have a world around them which teaches them slowly and gradually to conquer these lower powers and only then progress to higher powers.

That is the whole point of Earth evolution that human beings go through numerous lives on earth and in the rich and varied billowing wave movements gradually move towards perfection but in such a way that they learn to make their lower powers, instincts and longings serve higher ideas and issues. They would not be able to do this if at the time they first had to educate themselves to develop morality. They would not be able to do this if in the course of Earth evolution they had developed organs that let them have direct perception of electricity and magnetism. If they had, the temptation would have been too great to kill people whom for some reason or other they did not like, and allow only those who suited them to remain on earth.

We see, therefore, that it needs the spiritual point of view to make it possible for us to consider earthly existence from all angles and enter into it more deeply. When someone truly becomes this kind of spiritual investigator—we were only able to touch on it briefly yesterday[36]— they will truly enter into the spiritual world and find that there the higher hierarchies are around them just as here the three realms of nature are around them. There we get to know spirits which we call luciferic and ahrimanic. What kind of powers are the luciferic spirits? They are spirits which during the previous embodiment of the earth, in the old Moon period, lagged behind in their development, and did not enter into the complete hardening of earthly existence into which humanity entered. They remained at a level that preceded human development of a material nature. This meant that their powers continued to be more spiritual than those of humanity. Their evolution only took them to a level that is more spiritual than the level at which human beings go through their incarnations on earth. As they have brought their powers into human nature, this human nature has more spirituality in it than it was really supposed to have. If it had not been for these luciferic powers human beings would have personal spirituality in their unconscious powers, which are subordinate to the conscious powers of the I, powers like the luciferic ones, but not the powers which they do now have. Thanks to the luciferic powers, human beings have grown more spiritual in their lower nature than they would otherwise have been. They would have received everything they were meant to have on earth from the powers that are merely progressing, but they would not have been as spiritual as they are today. The luciferic element would be missing.

There is also something else which human beings would not have. Without this luciferic element humanity would not have known freedom, for without it they would have done everything in such a way that when there was something to be done they could have looked only at the ideas coming to them from the spiritual world. Whatever they would be doing on earth they would do in such a way that they would look to the idea behind it, like a picture that would show them what had to happen, and they would not need to create the idea for themselves. It would be like an inspiration from higher worlds, and this would be such a powerful influence that they could not possibly go against it. They would do the will of the gods, and it would be a matter of course.

But then there was the luciferic influence. This made it possible for human beings not simply to let the ideas for an action come to them from outside. Instead they had to do their own work from the deepest depths of their souls to develop their own ideas. They have to train themselves to think ethically, and this is something human beings would not be able to do if it had not been for the luciferic influence. This brought a more spiritual principle into our astral nature. The result is that not only the idea of morality, of ethics, is active in our I consciousness—its effect being that no one would think of doing anything evil for divine spirits would immediately put the idea of doing good things before the mind's eye—but so are our drives and passions active. This idea could not arise at all in our I consciousness if our astral nature, given individual character thanks to the luciferic influence, did not come to meet it. This luciferic influence has brought it about that there has to be purification in our nature, proceeding from the unconscious to the conscious mind, and we must work to develop conscious ethical ideas and motivation as we struggle against ourselves, and then follow those ethical concepts of our own free will. It is Lucifer, therefore, who makes it possible for us to follow ethical ideas once we have developed them ourselves.

Now we might say that there must after all be a power that arises from within us when we work our way up to ethical ideas. Where is this power in the human being, seeing that the individual is not ethical to begin with and has to train himself to be? Where is the power that works from the unconscious in the soul so as to put ethical ideas before him? Where is it within us, so that we may bring it out? Someone who as a spiritual investigator is able to look into the spiritual world will also discover where the power to produce ethical ideas is to be found. It is continually at work in the unconscious powers; it is there in the human being but is used for quite a different purpose in the ordinary world. When we act in the ordinary world, doing so before we have set ethical goals for ourselves, we are acting under the influence of our drives, desires and instincts. Yet we are only able to act by making our body act. There we are all the time working with unconscious powers, for who among those who have not been working with spiritual science knows which powers bend an arm, put one foot in front of the other, and so on? Without spiritual science we do not know what kind of powers these are that function in the human being. People do not know how their movements, everything which makes it possible for them to take action in the physical world around them, how this comes about and what power brings it about. The spiritual investigator will only get to know this when he achieves 'imaginative' insight, insight in images. You first of all create images for yourself. These take effect because they draw forth greater powers from the soul than those used in ordinary life. Whence comes this power which unfetters the images of imaginative inner life? It comes from the place where the powers are at work that make us able to take action in the world and let us move our hands and feet. This being the case, one will only achieve vision in images if one is able to be still, is able to bring the will of one's body to a standstill, to control it. One will then find that this power which otherwise moves one's muscles streams up into the sphere of soul and spirit and creates the images. One is repositioning those powers. Down there in the depths of the living body something exists of our very own being, something of which we are quite unaware in ordinary life. When we cut out the bodily element, the spirit which otherwise comes to expression in our actions rises up into the soul, filling it with this spirit which it must otherwise use for the bodily element. The spiritual investigator knows that he must deprive the body of something that the body normally consumes. For insight in images we must therefore cut out the bodily principle. In ordinary life we think, we form ideas, but in our organism the power to which we have been referring streams down into our organs when we are in waking consciousness, takes effect there, and as a rule is not at all used to being spiritually visible in the soul.

If we are not spiritual investigators we have no control of this power; we have to leave it down there in the subconscious. Yet it is doing something. It influences our moral or ethical ideas. When it streams upwards consciously, we train ourselves to gain insight in images using this power. If it is not consciously used for this, it serves us as we take action in the world. People are not always active, doing things; then this power which sits down there comes free, unconsciously, and is then also working to let ethical ideas arise. The very power, therefore, which moves our limbs, spiritually present in the living body so that people can take hold of things, walk and so on, frees itself in the human body at times and then produces our ethical and moral ideals. When we are able to admire someone who thinks ethical thoughts somewhere, developing noble ideas in solitude, we see the same powers coming free in those ideals which are involved in the movements of his hands and so on. To develop ethical ideals, a person must first be at rest, as it were.

We can, of course, also develop ethical ideals and then not follow them, for we also use the powers we use to develop those ideas to move around. They can be used for the one thing or the other. To develop ethical ideals does not yet mean to be ethical. You are only ethical in your actions if you follow those ideals. They then come up like memories. For as long as we must still train ourselves in them, we have to use the same energy to produce them as we later need to follow them. We have our ethical standards in us as remembered images. People must be trained to be ethical so that these images arise in them as their ethical standards and they are able to follow them.

Who is thus conjuring up these ethical ideals from our own nature within us? It is Lucifer. He compels us to produce our ethical ideas, our independent morality, out of our own resources. It is thanks to Lucifer that we have to do this. There is no freedom in the natural world. We find it only when we do bring to realization the element of spirit and soul within us. When Lucifer invaded the lower cravings of human beings he not only led humanity astray but also created human freedom. Lucifer's impulse made human beings free.

So if we study the inmost nature of our physical body in the way in which scientists study the natural world, and if we follow the laws of logic, we arrive at this source and origin of human freedom. If someone were to say today 'I don't believe in magnetism. I merely see a piece of iron and that cannot possibly attract another piece of iron. That's sheer fantasy,' this goes against life as it is lived. Yet in the sphere of soul and spirit people do behave in such a way that they deny the powers which exist. Luciferic powers are present in our freedom. Without them we could not be free, could never develop ethical impulses from the depths of our souls and follow them. We shall only really understand freedom when we realize that man's physical, sense-perceptible nature is imbued with an element of soul and spirit which does show itself in the movement of a hand but can free itself, consciously so in the spiritual scientist's vision in images, unconsciously in ethical ideals we put before us. Looking to our inner nature we also get to know Lucifer's good side, and are then no longer able to say that Lucifer is an evil spirit, for he is at the same time also the bringer of human freedom.

Human beings also change other powers in their souls so that they perform physical tasks, an example being speech, setting the speech organ in the brain in motion. There it is not the whole body in action but a matter of making the organization of the physical body perform actions, doing so from the sphere of soul and spirit; we are involved in an inner activity. When we speak, powers of soul and spirit intervene in Broca's area[37] which is in the third gyrus [convolution] of the brain and then in the larynx. When we grow aware of this power which acts on Broca's area, withdrawing it from speaking activity, as it were, and not using it for speech, we will have grasped it in its aspect of soul and spirit. Let us assume, for instance, that you meditate in such a way that you enter into the powers in your soul that are otherwise evident in speech but refrain from speech. You remain silent. If one thus stops the soul element within one, as it were, before it intervenes in the bodily sphere, one has grasped a power within one that leads to 'Inspiration', to spiritual hearing. The occult term 'silent perception' refers to this. It means the kind of silence where the powers which otherwise flow to the larynx are used inwardly. They penetrate into the soul sphere, making the soul active within. This is how one enters into the world of Inspiration.

Basically this world of Inspiration is a world entered into by the spiritual scientist which is separate from the world through which other spirits of the spiritual worlds make themselves known to us. In our cycle of time the situation is that as if from natural necessity, powers are more and more coming into play, unconsciously also in human beings, which otherwise only come into their own in the organs of the physical body and their inner activities.

When the power which people otherwise use in speech acts in them as though by nature, it enables them to perceive a spiritual principle, and this is equivalent to Inspiration. It is different from perceiving images with the eye of the true seer in image-based perception. This power, active in our ethical ideas, lets us see the good side of the luciferic spirits. If we are able to perceive things with the power which otherwise is used in speech we enter into the sphere which the Gospel of John

helps us to understand rightly by saying, without any religious prejudice: 'In the beginning was the Word.' We hear this 'Word' if we are
able to mute our own word, our own bodily nature, to such effect that
we arrest the power which normally speaks through the larynx before it
gets to the larynx and thus allow it to be free.

The obstacle responsible for the fact that human beings did not
perceive the world Word from the beginning was that they had to learn
to talk! However, as evolution continues, speech will turn into something that is very strange indeed. Speech and language have changed
greatly in the course of human evolution. If we go back to original levels
of speech, human beings were still directly connected with their speech.
Even today we find that country people are still much more alive and
active in speech, close to it. Saying a word, they still feel that something
like a reproduction of things they see around them is in that word. The
more human evolution progresses, the more abstract does the word
become, turning into a mere sign of what it is meant to express. Language is getting more and more inorganic, more and more arabesque-
like, more and more alien to people. What is the reason for this? This
process in which language grows remote from the inner meaning of
words reveals the powers which in the past were used to develop speech
and language. And this is because we shall soon have spiritual perception of the Christ spirit, exactly because the power to create speech
and language is coming free. In earlier times, language was closely
bound up with the human organism. Today it begins to become
emancipated from it. This frees the power that creates speech and
language, which will then be used to perceive the world Word, the
spiritual Christ.

We have now been considering two sides of human nature—how
human beings are on the one hand using the luciferic power to develop
their own ethical ideals and on the other hand gain the power to perceive the Christ in the spirit as the speech-generating power comes free,
that is, thanks to something they share with the whole of humanity,
since these powers come free within the whole of humanity. We come to
the Christ impulse because we are members of the whole human race.
To the same degree as language grows more and more abstract and the
power of speech becomes emancipated from the organism in human

nature, humanity is getting ready truly to perceive the Christ in the spirit. That is the other side of the coin with human evolution. Having grown more free inwardly under the luciferic influence which made it possible for them to develop their own ethical ideas, human beings will gain the ability—as though by a powerful outside influence—to connect with the Christ. The Christ will come to humanity by pouring his very essence out over the whole of human evolution as the quintessence of ethical ideas. Once it is known to the whole of humanity in this way, the Christ spirit will have something of the nature of moral principles. And there we come to something which shows that anthroposophy can rise to something that is able to combine the most sublime sense of truth with the noblest of moral principles. In my *Philosophy of Spiritual Activity*, completed 20 years ago, I sought to show that genuine freedom exists in the human soul when people follow the ethical principles they have brought to conscious awareness. What is the nature of these ethical principles? They do not compel us; we follow them of our own free will. A principle is never ethical if it compels. Principles we follow under compulsion have come to us from the outside world. Ethical principles can be identified by the fact that we are also free not to follow them. We have to be free in accepting their value. People only profess adherence to ethical and moral principles in a truly ethical way when they seek them out and the principles are not imposed on them. That is the characteristic of ethical principles. When human beings perceive him in the spirit, the Christ will have in common with ethical principles that one can also deny him, that he does not force anyone to recognize him. The old gods influenced other powers in the human soul. They still took hold of human beings in parts where they had not yet reached conscious awareness. The Christ, however, will appear to human beings consciously, in his spiritual nature, to the degree to which the individual has gained freedom in his conscious mind and will have risen to the Christ. He will be there for all who want to perceive him, though none will be forced to give him recognition. He will come to human beings in such a way that they will be able to follow of their own free will. Just as an ethical principle does not compel human beings but leaves them free to follow or not, so it will also be with the Christ spirit. Individual human beings must be fully aware of the value of this Christ spirit if they are prepared to follow him. Recognition given to the Christ spirit will in future also be a free deed in the soul. This will be something of infinite significance—that we may find our way to a truth which does not compel us to give recognition. We only give it recognition when we appreciate its full value.

The idea of Christianity given to us in anthroposophy—that it is still to come in its true form—will indeed provide a truth for human beings which in the most eminent sense is at the same time also a free truth. The following may be added, images which can then be more fully understood through meditation. One and the same word was used twice in human evolution, first with the temptation in Paradise, when Lucifer said to the human beings: 'Then your eyes shall be opened and you shall be as gods.'[38] That is Lucifer's impulse given as an image. Lucifer poured spirituality into the lower nature of man and at the same time made it possible for him to arrive at freedom through ethical principles. And the same word was used a second time when the Christ himself said: 'Is it not written in your law, I said, you are gods?'[39] The same word! We see that it is not only a matter of the meaning of a word but also of who says it, of the way in which a word is said. We see the necessary connection between Lucifer's deed and the Christ's deed, given in the form of an image, which is the way religious documents do it.

Lucifer is the bringer of personal freedom for the individual, the Christ is the bearer of freedom for the whole human race, all of humanity on earth. Anthroposophy significantly teaches us that acknowledgement of the Christ spirit will take the form that people are free to recognize the Christ or not, just as they are free not to be ethical.

The Christ is meant to be a truth the human soul is free to accept. All other truths belonging to the whole of humanity do compel us. But there are truths still resting in the world's keeping that relate specifically to the Mystery on Golgotha. Giving them recognition must be a free deed for the human spirit. They will give this spirit nobility in that they are acknowledged in an act of free will. Free truth, concrete free truth, deeply influences the human spirit as it evolves on earth. We see how gaining truth in freedom is one of the fundamental laws of human evolution.

We have seen that freedom could only enter into human evolution under the influence of Lucifer, and that initially human beings needed the help of this luciferic impulse so that they might rise to the truth. We may, however, see it as an ideal for the future that we can develop to gain freedom and freely acknowledge truths in the way presented here. Much could be said about anthroposophy, but it is unlikely that there is anything more closely connected with our need for freedom than what I have just been saying about free truth, something which must speak in the most profound and noble way of our human destiny.

We shall only feel what it means to be human on earth when we know the conscious ideal we have before us—the ideal of freedom and the truth, the truth which will create an external body for itself in that freedom.

I had to talk to you about such ideas of freedom at the very time when we have gained our own liberation as Anthroposophical Society,[40] released from bonds that had grown impossible, so that with these ideas we may sentiently give some indication of the kind of attitude one should altogether have in a society which makes such ideals the reason why we foregather.

In conclusion let me speak from my heart in telling you—and all the friends who have come from elsewhere to be here with our Swedish friends will share my feelings—how deeply satisfying it is, even more so as this event draws to its conclusion, that here, in this country, there is such profound, thoroughgoing understanding for the things I have been able to say, and for our aims in establishing the Anthroposophical Society. Truly, I choose these final words not to speak against something but to serve in the right way our freely developed anthroposophical ideal. May this Society, which you have established amongst you, contribute much still by way of work and effort to the things we were able to discuss today in this lecture on inner freedom perceived with anthroposophical insight. Let us hope that with this work the element will stream down that has existed for a long time in the spiritual worlds, waiting and hoping, and I am sure this will be so for us human beings if our work achieves things that will be so tremendously important for the development of humanity's spiritual endeavour. May this indeed be the work of this particular branch. And let these words be my farewell to you.

LECTURE 8

A number of friends have come from outside to join our friends under the Christmas tree here in Bochum and visit the branch of our spiritual searching that has been inaugurated here. I am sure that everyone who has come from elsewhere for the solemn inauguration of this branch appreciates the beauty and spiritual significance of the decision made by our Bochum friends to establish this centre for spiritual endeavour and spiritual feeling here in this city, in the midst of a centre of material activity, in a place which belongs mainly to external life, as it were. In many respects each and every one of our dear branches can be a symbol for us, more so in this region than anywhere else, for the significance of our kind of anthroposophical spiritual life in the present time and also for the future development of human souls.

When we find ourselves in the midst of a field of most modern material activity, this is not something we should criticize or denigrate, for it is indeed a region which shows us how things must come to be more and more in external life on earth as time goes on. We would be lacking in sense if we were to say, 'Let the old times return when people had woods and meadows around them, as it were, and the original life of nature rather than the chimneys we see in our day.' That would show lack of sense. For we would demonstrate that we have no insight into 'the eternal necessities into which man must find his way', as wise men of all times would say. Material life spread over the earth especially in the nineteenth century and will do so even more comprehensively in times to come. And there can be no criticism of this kind of life where one is in sympathy with earlier times. No, we have to realize that this is the destiny of our planet earth. From a certain point of view one may call the old days good, considering them to have been like the springtime or summertime on earth, but to rant and rave because times change would be just as senseless as it would be to be dissatisfied because spring and summer are followed by autumn and winter. So we have to appreciate and love it when our friends have resolved, with real courage, to create a centre for our spiritual life right among the hustle and bustle of the most modern life. And it will be good if all who have come to visit here for just one day go away with heart-felt gratitude for the good work our Bochum friends are doing in a truly spiritual-scientific way.

What I think is so good about the inauguration of new branches through the years is that friends come from outside, often a long way, on such occasions to be with the people who have come together in a particular place. It means that these friends from outside can first of all light the inner fire of their gratitude from direct experience, a fire we must have for all the people who establish such branches, and that on the other hand these friends can take with them a lively memory of the event. This will keep alive the thoughts we send from all around to the work of such a branch, so that their work may bear fruit thanks to creative thoughts from all directions. For we know that life in the spirit is a reality, we know that thoughts are not just what materialists believe them to be but are live powers. And when we lovingly unite our thoughts about some place where we are active in this way those thoughts can unfold there and be a help.

I think we may be sure that those who have visited here today will also take home with them the impulse to think many, many times of this our work, so that our friends here in Bochum may feel, as they sit quietly together, entering deeply into the spiritual insights granted to us by the hierarchies, that creative thoughts come to them from all sides as they meet here in their centre, their centre for spiritual work.

Our anthroposophical view of life gradually teaches us to see things as they are and not to be unjustifiably critical of life as it is. Undoubtedly we have to admit to ourselves that the earth is going through an evolution. And if we, equipped with our anthroposophical knowledge or even just sensibly using the knowledge that exists outside anthroposophy look back on earlier times in Earth evolution, then, compared to an earth furrowed by railways, with telegraph wires everywhere, with electrical currents passing through it everywhere, earlier times seem to us to be times of spring and summer, whilst the times ahead of us seem like the autumn and winter of our earth. But it is not for us to complain about this. No, it is something we must call a necessity. It is not for us to complain, just as it is not right for people to complain when summer comes to an end and autumn and winter lie ahead.

Centuries ago the human soul would prepare itself when autumn and winter did come to set up the sign for the living Word entering into Earth evolution in the depth of winter's night. And with this the human heart, the human soul, showed that the living principle that summer provides without human beings doing anything must now be created by human beings doing something out of their inner being.

The shooting and sprouting powers of spring delight us and so do the gentle powers of summer without having to do anything to produce them—evidence year after year that divine and spiritual powers reign in the world. When winter covers those joys with snow and darkness and cold prevail we do in the midst of winter hold on to the summery hope for the future that comes in winter, a hope that tells us that just as spring and summer will follow every winter, so there will be a new spiritual spring and summer one day, when the earth will have achieved its goal, and our own creative powers will help to shape them. Thus the human heart sets up for itself the sign of everlasting life.

It is in this sign of spiritual life everlasting that we feel united today with our Bochum friends as we formally inaugurate the branch they established here some time ago. It is good to be able to do this just before Christmas.

It may well be that some people listen only superficially to all the things our spiritual science discovers about Christ Jesus, the things revealed about Christ Jesus. Taking a superficial point of view, it may perhaps seem to them that we are replacing the simplicity and childlike nature of Christmas, bringing to mind the beautiful scenes from Matthew's and Luke's Gospels, with something tremendously complicated. We need to make the human soul aware that at the beginning of our era *two* Jesus children entered into Earth evolution.[41] We have to speak of the way in which the I of the one Jesus child entered into the bodies of the other; we have to say that in the thirtieth year of Jesus' life the Christ spirit came down and lived for three years in the bodies of Jesus of Nazareth. It may well seem that all the love, the deep feeling which human beings knew how to develop for centuries, for their salvation, when they were shown the Jesus child in the manger, surrounded by the shepherds, when their ears heard the wonderful, deeply touching carol, when Christmas plays were celebrated in many places, when the candles shone on the Christmas tree, gladdening their hearts, it may well seem that compared to all this, which immediately ignites human hearts as they are beheld, arousing deep feelings, piety and love—that compared to all this the warmth of feeling, of sentience, had to die away if one must first take up the more complicated ideas of the two Jesus children, of the I of one of them entering into the bodies of the other, of a divine and spiritual principle entering into the bodies of Jesus of Nazareth. Yet we must not give way to such thoughts, for it would be dreadful if we were not willing to accept the law of necessity in this area.

Yes, my friends, in villages out there on the edge of the woods or among fields and meadows, villages to which the snow-covered mountains and far distant places would speak or the vast plains and lakes, in villages where no railway lines or telegraph wires were to be seen—there hearts could live that would immediately light up when the nativity was set up and people were reminded of the story of the birth of that lovely infant, as told by Matthew or Luke. Those stories of what happened on earth, stories that bear witness of the event, live and will live on. But a time which enters into 'earth's winter', as we may well call it, a time of railways, telegraph wires and tall chimneys, needs greater strength in the soul if hearts are to catch fire and develop deep feelings in spite of external mechanics, materiality. The soul must grow strong and be so convinced inwardly that everything that happened to prepare for the Mystery on Golgotha is true, that all of it lives firmly in the heart, however much the mechanical natural order may intervene in earthly existence. News of the child would have come in a different way to the people who lived on the edge of the wood, on mountain slopes, by the lakes and among fields and meadows than it must now come to those who must be able to deal with the conditions of life in more recent times.

This is the reason why the Masters of Wisdom and the Harmony of Sentience are today telling us something we must take into account when we speak of the child in Bethlehem. Our hearts are then no less full as we behold the Christmas tree, in spite of having to have knowledge today which people of earlier times did not have. Quite the contrary, we gain a better understanding of those earlier times; we come to see why hope for the future and joy certain for the future shone in the eyes of young and old by the Christmas tree and the manger. We come to understand that in those days more was alive in this than people were able to see in such a direct way if we consider the reasons in our mind why we feel such deep, inward love for the child of Bethlehem. In the best, the very best sense we may call the one of the Jesus children who was descended from the Nathan line in the house of David 'the child of humanity, the child of man'. For what do we feel for this child whose spirit still shines out from the words in the Gospel of Luke?

The human race had its origin with the earth's origin. It has gone through much in Lemurian, Atlantean and post-Atlantean times. And we know that this was a decline, that at the times of origin the human race had original knowledge and vision, an original bond with the divine and spiritual powers, an ancient legacy of knowing of the bond with the gods. Everything coming from the gods which thus lived in human souls came to be toned down more and more as time went on. In the course of time human beings had less and less immediate awareness of their connection with the divine and spiritual ground and origin. They were progressively cast out, as it were, into the field of sheer material vision, existence in the senses. It was only in the beginnings of life, in infancy, that people knew to venerate innocence, to love the innocence of a human being who had not yet taken in the earth's powers of decline.

But as we now know, a spirit came down to earth with one of the Jesus children who had not been on earth before, a soul which had not gone through humanity's evolution on earth—I have written of this in my *Occult Science, an Outline*—and had been held back, as it were, in the state of innocence prior to Lucifer's temptation. Such a soul, childlike in a much, much higher sense than one usually thinks, came to earth. And how could we not recognize it as 'the child of the human race'? The child who came to earth as Luke's Jesus child shows something which we human beings may no longer show, not even at the most tender age of infancy, something which we cannot perceive in any of us, not even at the moment when we first open our eyes in the earth's realm. For this child had a soul that had not been born from a human body on earth before, which had remained behind when human evolution on earth took a new beginning, appearing on an earth wholly in its childhood stage at the beginning of our era. Hence the wondrous thing revealed to us in the Akashic Record,[42] that this child, the Nathan Jesus child, produced speech sounds immediately after being born which only his mother could understand. Those sounds were not like any of the languages spoken at that time, nor at any time, but something came to the mother from them that was like a message from worlds that are not earthly, from higher worlds. That is the wondrous thing, that this Jesus child was able to speak as soon as he was born.

The child then grew up as if he had to have in his own inner nature a concentrate of everything which all human souls together could produce by way of life and capacity for love, as it were. It was the great geniality of love which lived in the child. He was not able to learn much of what human civilization had achieved in life on earth. Up to his twelfth year, the Nathan Jesus child knew little of the things humanity had achieved in the course of millennia. Because he was unable to do so, the other I entered into him in his twelfth year. But all the things he had touched on from his earliest, most tender childhood onwards were touched by love brought to perfection. All the qualities of mind, all qualities of feeling, were as if heaven had sent love to earth, so that a light might be borne into the wintertime on earth, a light to shine in the darkness of the human soul in winter when the sun does not unfold its outer strength to the full. When the Christ later entered into the bodies of this human being, we have to remember that this Christ spirit could only make itself understood on earth because it had to act by going through those bodies.

The Christ spirit is not a human being. It is a spirit from the higher hierarchies. On earth it had to live as a human being among human beings for three years. For this, a human being had to be born who was the way I have often described for the Nathan Jesus child. Not having been on earth before, and therefore lacking the education of previous incarnations, this child of man could not have taken in the fruits of external civilization on earth. A soul therefore entered into this child who had in the highest sense gained for himself everything external civilization can give—the Zarathustra soul.

So we see the most admirable state of affairs when we have Christ Jesus before us. We see how this child of man, who had saved humanity's best expectation for earth—love—from the times when human beings had not yet succumbed to luciferic temptation, until the beginning of our era when he appeared for the first time in a human body on earth. He worked together with Zarathustra, humanity's most highly developed prophet. The great spirit, whose true home had until the Mystery on Golgotha been within the realms of the higher hierarchies, then had to appear on earth, entering earth existence through the gate of Jesus of Nazareth's bodies. The child of man brought with him to the highest degree something which is only hinted at in the purity seen in the eyes of an innocent child. The most sublime achievement possible on earth—this is something which Zarathustra gave to this child of man. And the Christ spirit gave to the earth what the heavens can give it—that it might be receptive in the spirit for what is given to it every summer when the powers of the sun increase.

We will just have to come to understand everything that has happened to the earth. And for the times that lie ahead the soul will be able to gain in inner depth, grow strong thanks to a power that will be greater than all the powers that have so far joined up with the Mystery on Golgotha, and this at a time where outwardly little support is given for the powers to gain strength that tend towards true human powers of source and origin, their inmost nature, so that human beings may understand how this spirit comes from the cosmic world of the spirit. Yet if we are to understand this fully we must first rise to the kind of understanding that people once had of the Jesus child on Christmas Day, to perception of the spirit. There will be times when people will look at events on earth with the eyes of the soul, as it were. They will then say many things to themselves which we cannot yet say to ourselves today in so many situations, something made possible only by spiritual science today. We are already able to say many things to ourselves that cannot yet be mentioned in many, many situations.

We see spring coming, plants shooting and sprouting from the ground. We feel joy coming alight as we see this. We feel the power of the sun increase up to the point where it makes our bodies jubilant, up to the St John's sun which was celebrated in the Nordic mysteries. The initiates of those mysteries knew that at St John's tide the sun pours out warmth and light over the earth, revealing cosmic activity around the earth's periphery. We see and feel all this.

We do, of course, also see and feel other things during this time. Lightning and thunder may crash into the rays of the spring sun when clouds cover them. Rain pours down irregularly. And we then sense the infinite, harmonious regularity of the sun's progress that cannot be influenced by anything, and the—well, let us use the word—capricious activities of entities that have an influence on earth in the form of rain and sunshine, thunderstorms and other phenomena that depend on all kinds of irregular things, in contrast to the regular, harmonious influence of the sun's progress and its consequences for plant development and everything else that lives on earth. Infinitely regular harmony of sun activity and the capriciousness of things happening in our immediate atmosphere. We are aware of there being two things.

But when autumn approaches we feel that living things are dying, things we enjoy are withering away. And if we have a feeling for nature, our souls may well feel sad as nature is dying. The awakening, loving power of the sun, something moving through the universe in regular harmony disappears from view, as it were, and capriciousness gains the day. It is true, and people still knew of this in earlier times, though we no longer have it in mind in our materiality—in winter earth's egotism gains the victory over powers that stream down to our earth from far-away world existence, penetrating our atmosphere and awakening life on our earth.

And so the whole of outside nature seems to us to involve two things. Spring and summer activity, utterly different from autumn and winter activity, is as if the earth were growing selfless—giving itself up to the embrace of the universe, with the sun sending it light and warmth and awakening life. The earth in spring and summer appears to show self-lessness. The earth in autumn and winter seems to reveal egotism, conjuring up out of itself all it is able to contain and produce in its own atmosphere. Overcoming the sun's activity, cosmic activity, with the egotism of earthly activity—that seems to be the earth in winter.

And when we look away from the earth and at ourselves with the eye which spiritual investigation opens for us, when we look altogether beyond the material and to the spiritual, we see something else as well. We do know that elemental spirits live in all that goes on around us in the struggles of spring and summer, looking as if only the capricious forces of the earth's atmosphere influenced the unfolding sun powers. Countless spirits, lower ones and higher ones, are active in the elemental realm around the earth. Lower spirits, earthbound in the elemental realm, have to put up with higher spirits streaming down from the universe to be much more dominant, making them the servants of the spirits that stream down from the sun, making the demonic powers that prevail in the egotism of earth itself serve them. In spring and summer on earth we see the spirits of earth, air, water and fire made to serve the cosmic spirits that send their powers down to the earth. If we understand the whole spiritual situation of earth and cosmos our souls are given up to these relationships in spring and summer, saying to ourselves: 'Earth, you are showing yourself to us by making the spirits that serve egotism serve the universe, serve the cosmic spirits that conjure up life from your womb, a life that you yourself would not be able to conjure up.'

We then move towards autumn and winter. And we sense the egotism of the earth, sense how powerful those spirits of the earth grow that are bound to this earth, spirits that have separated from the universe from Saturn, Sun and Moon times, sense how they isolate themselves from the influences coming from the cosmos. We feel ourselves to be in an earth that is egotistically living for itself. And we may then perhaps look in ourselves. We test our soul in its thinking, feeling and will, test it in all seriousness, asking ourselves: 'How do thoughts come up from deep down in our soul? How do our feelings, affects and sentience come up? Do they show the regularity which the sun shows as it moves through the universe, providing the earth with vital energies conjured up from its womb?' They do not. The powers evident in our everyday thinking, feeling and will are even in their outer aspect similar to the capricious goings-on in the atmosphere. Human passions irrupt into the soul just as thunder and lightning irrupt. Human thoughts follow no law as they rise from the depths of the soul just as rain and sunshine are not subject to any law. Superficially we do have to compare our inner life with the way in which wind and weather change, not showing the regularity with which the sun rules our earth. Out there, spirits of air and water, spirits of fire and earth are active in the elemental realm, and it is they which really represent the egotism of our earth. Within ourselves, elemental powers do the same. But these changing powers in us that regulate our everyday life are embryos, seeds that are mere germs, but these germs nevertheless resemble the elemental spirits that prevail in all the capriciousness out there. As we think, feel and do things we bear within us the powers of the same world, powers that live as demonic spirits in the elemental realm in wind and weather out there.

In times when the people who were at the turning point between the old and the new times felt 'a time is coming that reminds us of earth's winter time' there were teachers among those people, sages who knew how to interpret the signs of the times and make people aware: 'Though our inner life is much like the capricious activities in the outside world, we human beings do know that behind this activity in the outside world, especially in autumn and winter, the sun does shine, is alive and active in the universe and will return.' And people may also cling to the thought that compared to their own capricious inner life there is a sun, deep, deep down in the depths where the wellspring of our soul bubbles forth from the wellspring of the world itself. The sages made people aware at the turning point of time that just as the sun must return and gain power again to overcome earth's egotism, so insight will have to be gained from the depths of our soul for anything that can come to this soul from those wellsprings, where the soul's life is directly connected with the spiritual sun in the world, just as life on earth is connected with the physical sun in the world.

This sounded like a hope when it was said, referring to the great symbol presented by nature herself. And so the winter solstice was made a festival for the days when the sun would gain strength again. They said to themselves of this time: 'Whichever way the earth's egotism may unfold, the sun gains the victory over earth's egotism. The spirits coming from the sun penetrate into the world of the elemental spirits which represent earth's egotism as if through the darkness of a holy night, showing us how they make the egotistical spirits of the earth serve them.'

At first it seemed a hope. And when the great turning point of time had come, when otherwise desolation and emptiness would have had to arise in human souls, the Mystery on Golgotha was in preparation. In the sphere of the spirit it was evident that powers do indeed live within human beings that can only be compared with the capricious powers of the earth atmosphere, with the earth's egotism. These were evident in the old days when people still had an heirloom from the old powers of the gods in them, like the powers that appear in spring and summer—servants of the old hierarchies of the gods. But as the time of the Mystery on Golgotha approached the inner powers of human souls came to be more and more like the external demonic elementals in autumn and winter. These powers of ours were to tear themselves away from the old streams of the gods, the old influences, just as in winter the capricious powers of our earth withdraw from sun activity. Then it happened in humanity's evolution on earth, as people had always hopefully envisaged symbolically in the sun's victory over the powers of winter. The world winter solstice came, with the spiritual sun going through the same thing as the physical sun always went through at the winter solstice, going through this for the whole of Earth evolution. And the Mystery on Golgotha came in those times.

We must make clear distinction between two different periods of time on earth: the time before the Mystery on Golgotha, moving through earth's summer and towards its autumn, with the inner powers of human beings coming to resemble the capricious powers of the earth more and more; and the great feast of the earth's Christmas, the time of the Mystery on Golgotha, when earth's winter did indeed befall the earth. But out of the darkness the victorious spirit of the sun, the Christ, approached the earth, inwardly bringing to souls the powers of growth which the sun brings to the earth in the outside world.

Standing by the Christmas tree we are very much aware, therefore, of the whole of our human destiny on earth, our inmost human nature. We feel close to the child of man that brought a message across from the time when humanity had not yet fallen into temptation and thus the potential of decline, of descent, a message that there would be a new beginning again, as the ascent begins with the winter solstice. It is on that very day that we are really aware of the close connection which the spiritual element in the inner soul has with the spirit that is present and active in everything, coming to outer expression in wind and weather, and also in the regular, harmonious progress of the sun, and to inward expression in the progress of humanity over the earth, in the great Golgotha festival.

Following these thoughts—which should not remain thoughts but turn into feelings and sentiment—humanity surely needs to develop a new religiosity, intimate and inward, a religiosity that cannot be blunted even in the face of the most extreme mechanization which must inevitably develop on earth. Surely it should be possible again to have Christmas prayers, Christmas carols, even in an earth atmosphere that has grown abstract, filled with telegraph wires and smoke, when people will learn to feel how they are connected with the divine and spiritual powers in their depths, having a feeling deep down in themselves for earth's great Christmas festival at the birth of the St Luke Jesus child?

It is true indeed, and on the one hand one could hear it through the whole of human history on earth, that one day there had to come the earth's great Christmas festival, preparing for the Easter festival on Golgotha. It is true indeed that this unique event had to come as the sun spirit's victory over the capricious earth spirits. On the other hand, Angelus Silesius[43] was right in saying: 'The Christ could be born a thousand times in Bethlehem—but all in vain lest he is born in me.' It is indeed true that we have to find the element in those depths of our soul that allows us to understand Christ Jesus.

But it is also true that after a summer spent in the fields and pastures the people who lived on the edges of the woods, at the lakeside, or surrounded by mountains and were able to look towards the symbol of the Christ child felt something different in their souls than we do, we who must feel strong enough to receive the Christmas message even in a time that has become mechanized and abstract, smoke-filled and dry. If these powerful thoughts which spiritual science can give us can take root in our hearts, a sun power will come from these hearts of ours that will be capable of shining into the most desolate outside environment with a power that will be as if within ourselves light upon light were ignited on the tree of our inner life. The roots of this tree are the roots of our soul itself, and in this winter season we must do more and more to transform it into the Christmas tree. We can do this if we take the message of the spirit, which true anthroposophy can be for us, not just as theory but as something that is full of life. This is how I wanted to bring the thoughts of Christmas from our spiritual science into the room we want to inaugurate today for the work which our friends have already been doing here for some time.

Our friends here want to dedicate their work and their branch to a god who in the north is considered to be the god who brings rejuvenating powers, spiritual childhood powers, to a human race that is growing old. Nordic people turn to this god when they want to speak of something which, coming from the Christ Jesus spirit, can bring new tidings to our human race of rejuvenation. His is the name to which our friends want to dedicate their work and their branch. They want to call it the Vidar Branch. May this name hold promise, just as the work done here, what has already been done by people who love the spirit and intend to do in time to come holds promise for us. Let us truly appreciate what our Bochum friends here are attempting, and let us bless the work, also calling for the Christ's blessing, by unfolding our best and most loving thoughts here for the blessing, the power and the genuine, true spiritual love for this work. We can feel that we are celebrating today's festival of naming the Vidar Branch in the right sense.

And let our feelings rise to those whom we call the guides and leaders of our spiritual life, to the Masters of Wisdom and the Harmony of Sentience, and ask their blessings on the work that is to grow and develop in this city through our friends.

> You who guide life in the spirit and give to humanity
> what human beings need, according to their time,
> you are joining in when our friends in this city
> devotedly serve that life in the spirit.

Let us send this prayer to the spiritual leaders, the higher hierarchies, at this moment which is a solemn one in two respects. And we may hope that the promise which lies in the work done in this branch will win through, in spite of all resistance that is growing apace, in spite of all obstacles and opposition—that with it the Christ secret may be embodied anew in humanity in the way that it needs to happen.

Let it be our Christmas prayer today that this may happen: that this branch, too, may be a living witness of the power that comes to human evolution from higher worlds, making human souls more and more aware of the truth in the following words:

> They speak to our senses
> The things in far-off spaces,
> Changing within the stream of time;
> With insight, human souls
> Enter into the sphere of things eternal,
> Free of the boundaries of space
> And untouched by the stream of time.

Our friends here in Bochum will proceed with the work, their hearts full of this feeling, as will be the hearts of those of us who have been present here and will know of their work, thinking of it many, many times. These thoughts can gain great strength because we have been able to add our blessing to this work immediately before this year's Christmas festival. This can be a symbol to us for everything victorious over the material world, over all opposition that may and will somehow arise in the world.

LECTURE 9

It may so easily seem that the simple, loving joy that lived for such a long time in hundreds upon hundreds of hearts when people saw such a play of the divine infant[44] and his destiny on earth—that this joy may be diminished by our spiritual-scientific philosophy with what appear to be highly complex insights, bringing in so much information about Christ Jesus, insights we must seek to gain in our philosophy of life. I am sure that every heart, every mind feels great joy when we see such a play and can be aware again that for centuries the hearts of people in cities and in isolated rural areas, those who have gone through a degree of cultural life as well as those who have remained simple country folk, have felt strongly drawn to the divine infant. They perceived powers in him that entered into human evolution at a point in time, saving it from the death in the spirit which was considered to be inevitable due to an eternal cosmic law. Every heart, every mind must be touched when people see once again how this divine infant was venerated in the past.

Yet it is only seemingly the case that more detailed and complex insight into the miracle at Bethlehem would somehow diminish this immediate warmth, this elemental feeling. I am saying that anyone who can say such a thing has only taken a superficial view of these things. For we do face a different world today from hundreds of years ago when people did not see those Christmas plays as something remembered but as something that was simply part of their everyday life. This complicated time of ours, with so many elements of scientific thinking, needs a different inner impulse if we are to look up again to the divine infant who brought the greatest impulse into human evolution. Our particular approach,[45] speaking of the two Jesus children, the Solomonic and the Nathan child, only seems to be more complicated. For in the Nathan child we see that when the rest of humanity set out for life on earth this child of all humanity, as it were, the human being remained behind in spiritual worlds before the tempter, the luciferic principle, approached human beings. We see that this child was kept at the level of humanity's infancy, as it were, held back as humanity's spiritual childhood impulse until 'the days were accomplished', and was then born as an exceptional human being, the Nathan Jesus child. He came to earth as a human I that had not gone through previous incarnations on earth but entered into earthly embodiment for the first time. As soon as he was born he spoke to his mother in a language only she was able to understand, a language that seemed to come down from heavenly heights.[46]

We will come to realize more and more that at a time when the human being is seen in such a different light we will need to look up to the divine infant whom we venerate as the Nathan Jesus child who remained behind at humanity's childhood level in spirit land, was born with the human qualities, those original qualities which all human beings would have had if luciferic temptation had not taken them into Earth evolution. The Nathan Jesus child entered the human race with all the qualities that humanity had before they yielded to luciferic temptation.

We need to know this today, we must know that in this Jesus child we have the childhood of the whole of humanity. We can then from the deepest depths of our soul share in the feelings of those simple people in the past. They could only feel, as they saw the glorification of the divine infant in those plays, what we are now able to know if we are prepared to take the road to the spirit. Our souls are most deeply touched when in a play such as the one we have just seen we are aware of the infant's profound innocence, the divine innocence of a child, something which humanity had before the tempter changed this. The tempter takes the form of Lucifer, and later Ahriman, whom we must consider to be the 'devil' of medieval times. The contrast touches us deeply between Herod led astray by the devil and Herod taken by the devil on the one hand

and the child of man who preserved the principle of human innocence and will lead us to life eternal.

Ideas like these, as they live in such a play, truly had not come from superficial feelings. They had come from the intuitive perception of the most profound secrets of the world. In medieval times people everywhere, in towns as well as in the most desolate mountain and country regions, would recognize this, even if only vaguely. But in the past, human souls approached those secrets in a way that differs from the way in which we must come to fathom them again.

The inner eye will easily turn from such a play to presentations made with all the means of truly sublime art in the thirteenth and fourteenth centuries as they arose from the fullness of Christian feeling, showing the whole secret of human evolution across the globe and the way in which the human soul relates to the eternal divine element in human nature. And today, when we are about to celebrate Holy Night in our own way, I want to turn from these plays to a magnificent presentation which holds the very ground and origin in it of what is also to be found in those simple plays.

In Pisa, in western Italy, is the famous cathedral where Galilei[47] observed the swinging lamp which made his genius discover the laws without which modern physics would be unthinkable. Next to the cathedral is the famous Camposanto cemetery, surrounded by high walls. There medieval artists recorded what people were thinking about the divine secrets and the connection of human beings with those secrets, with the eternal soul principle which they thought to be part of human nature. Many of those medieval secrets are depicted on the walls of the Camposanto in Pisa. In those times God's acre would be covered with soil which the crusaders had brought back from the tomb of Christ Jesus. Anyone who visits this cemetery today and picks up a handful of soil may well feel that under this soil lies something which the crusaders once brought with them from Palestine and spread on this God's acre which was thought to be particularly sacred.

One of the paintings on the Camposanto walls is *The Triumph of Death*.[48] It was, however, only given that name in 1705. Before that everyone who saw it and knew it and spoke of it called it *Purgatory*. And we can be certain that there was also a 'heaven' and a 'hell' on those

The Triumph of Death by Francesco Traini

cemetery walls. This *Purgatory* shows in the most profound way how people of medieval times saw the secret of the human soul and its connection with the eternal in man. Much of the painting has perished today. But it is still possible to see through the damage and understand the great secrets of evolving humanity which the painter, not known to history, wanted to conjure up on the cemetery wall.

We first of all see a procession of kings and queens coming out of something like a cave in a mountain, full of self-awareness and arrogance, and of the feeling: We know what it means to have this status on earth. The procession emerges from a mountain cave and as it emerges comes upon three coffins guarded by a hermit. So the hunting party suddenly finds itself faced with three coffins. And what lies in those coffins is characteristically different. One contains a skeleton, one a corpse which has decomposed to the point where worms are feeding on it, and the third holds someone who has died recently, having only just started to decompose. The procession comes to a halt. A hermit is sitting in front of the coffins, his gesture appearing to say: 'Stop! Let this grim reminder, this *memento mori*, make you see what you really are as human beings.' Higher up, above the mountain, on another rising slope we see three hermits, hermits who get food, and also hermits bent low over books and reflecting on the secrets of human development. The whole is arranged in such a way that one mountain forms the ceiling, as it were, up above. Above the point where the hunting party comes upon the coffins are the three hermits who represent peace and have the power to enter into the inmost human soul, there to find the connection of this human soul with the Elysian Fields. As we go on looking we see all kinds of sick people jumbled together directly behind the hunting party who have stopped at the *memento mori*. We also see people listening to a harp, and behind the harp a figure putting a finger to the mouth. And above it all we see masses of angelic spirits crowding on one side and horrible images of devilish spirits on the other. The painter has used all his powers of imagination to create those devils. On the right side of the whole painting we see angels bending down to the human beings who are listening to the harp. Between them and the mountain which has fire coming from its crater we see the devils evolving.

All this is really there to direct the eye to something which one might perhaps fail to note at first sight. Yet it will gradually provide insight into the most profound secrets relating to humanity. What was really meant to be shown there? Well, it is typical for the view held by medieval scholars to see the hunting party stopping at the three dead bodies—a skeleton, a corpse on which worms are feeding, and the bloated body of someone who has recently died. It is a theme often seen in medieval works. We will only understand it if we ask: Why are the people coming out of a mountain? Who are the people in the hunting party?—and if we know that they are not alive; they are dead people who are in kamaloka. 'Your bodies are like this,' the painting says, 'the skeleton as your physical body, the corpse eaten by worms as your ether body, and the one belonging to someone who has just died as your astral body. Remember, you who are in life, what you are shown here of the secrets of existence after death.' This is how the secret of the three human bodies was shown in medieval times.

Strange, marvellous, one would like to say. The hermit sitting slightly elevated in front of the coffins makes a gesture which indicates that humanity does need to penetrate into the secrets of existence, so that we may realize how we are connected with the eternal wellsprings for our transitory existence. The painting then continues in such a way that above it all the mountain rises, with the hermits sitting up there in quiet contemplation and a natural world full of peace, showing us as it were how one can connect with the inner essence of human nature by being contemplative.

This is what the painter sought to show, and not a *Triumph of Death*, which is the name given to the painting at a later time, when it was no longer understood. We can see how right the people were who spoke of purgatory, that is, of kamaloka, as we call it. The painter wanted to show that when we are in life we are not always among those who perceive the significance of life after death and have the right attitude to the eternal principle in human nature. He showed this in people who are no longer in life but in the life after death, for the members of the hunting party are people who are in kamaloka; they are already dead. And on the other hand we see how the devils and the angels take away human souls. We see the profundity, with every devil having a soul in its claws and taking it away, and every angel taking a soul under its wings. But these souls differ from one another, and that is what I would wish to mention now at Christmas time. The souls taken by the devils— misshapen, justifiably so, but created with real insight—are souls that look like older people. And those taken to the Elysian Fields by the angels are souls which the painter showed as children. We sense there the view, which was held throughout the Middle Ages, that there is something in human beings that must remain childlike for the whole of earth existence, with people preserving something for themselves however old and decrepit they may grow—child-nature, innocence of feeling—for the whole of life, and on the other hand that there are people who grow old not just outwardly, physically, but also mentally because they take up earthly mentality. For it is only on earth that we grow old. People who grow old in that sense can only do so by their own fault, by something that makes them look away from the heavenly and eternal. That is why their souls look like people who have grown old, whilst the souls of those who stay connected with the element that preserves the connection with the eternal in the spiritual world retain their childlike form.

This is what is so great, so tremendous in this painting in the Camposanto in Pisa, telling us that there is something in human nature of which we must see that it reflects the eternal principle in man in the first three years of childhood, something I have tried to show in the small volume *The Spiritual Guidance of Man and Humanity*.[49] I sought to show that human beings are indeed different in the first three years of childhood from what they are later in life. In medieval times people really felt that close link with the divine and spiritual heights which belonged to childhood. And it was shown in a work of art as magnificent as this one, perhaps the most interesting painting of earlier times considering its composition. It was so great that people ascribed it to Giotto[50] and various other painters of his time, though that is impossible because it was painted at a later period. This painting shows most gloriously how medieval people related to the child. It is the kind of sentience we find everywhere. We see it so marvellously in these simple plays telling of the Christ child; we see it in the fact that the very legend of the Jesus child found a home in all hearts, with infinite warmth, and how this legend of the child actually made people know how they are connected with the Christ impulse. People needed to be certain that the principle which will save eternity for the human soul has come with that child. Just as someone who has preserved his eternal part is taken to the Elysian Fields by the angels is shown as a child in the painting, one must also imagine that with the form of the innocent infant there came into the world the one of whom we know that he united with the divine Christian impulse, with the divine Christ spirit in the thirtieth year of his life.

Here, I'd say, we have the connection between the heights of spiritual life in medieval times, as depicted in the painting in Pisa's Camposanto, and the simple plays. The plays we have been seeing here only came into existence at a later time, but all of them have the impulses in them that reflect what we are now again looking for in the tone and character of our own time. And the relationship that human souls had to the Jesus child was not just 'simple'—which is what people are often told today. Here we have been hearing of the Nathan Jesus child who in his twelfth year received the Zarathustra I into himself and in his thirtieth year the Christ spirit, and we must understand this if we are to bring to mind what had to happen in human evolution so that humanity might save the eternal principle which is part of them. In medieval times people did not need all the knowledge that is presented in concepts and theories; they had the magnificent visions of the nature of the human soul like the one in the painting we have been considering. Other times call for other ways of showing the secrets of eternity, and this has been done in different ways through the ages. Again and again it manifests that human beings may have great hopes for their souls. Before the Mystery on Golgotha it was the hope that there was to come something which in the human being is spiritual and corresponds to the physical sun in our planetary system. Today we are able to know the very thing that has been so deeply felt at all times.

In spring we see life, the plants, shoot and sprout from the ground and watch them grow towards summer. We turn our eyes to the sun and know: The powers that make the earth fruitful come from the sun, so that the active life of shooting and sprouting plants and all kinds of creatures may arise from the soil. And apart from this, which happens in sacred order year after year, we see the regularity of the sun's progress, bringing the blessing it needs to take to every place on earth at the given hour, but also things entering into this that may be said to belong to the earth's atmosphere—gales sweeping across the fields, rain pouring from the clouds, mists spreading across the landscape. There we see something that does not follow a regular order. We may see regularity and order in anything that comes from the sun. In spring and summer we feel, as we look at nature, that the sun, victorious as it hastens across the earth, is capable of influencing the winds and weather on the earth's surface. But when autumn approaches and when winter is coming, with the sun losing its strength and not intervening so much in earth existence, we become aware in a different way of the capricious nature of earth's own activities. Anyone who considers this alternation between spring and summer on the one hand and autumn and winter on the other in a reflective way will be able to say to himself: In spring the sun gains the victory with its sacred order over the changeable conditions which the earth's egotism brings forth from earth nature. But winter is the time when the earth produces the effects in its egotistical atmosphere, when earth nature gains the victory over the blessings that come down to earth from the cosmos.

Reflecting on our inner life—thinking, feeling and doing[*]—we see how feeling impulses, affects, the powers of will rise up without regularity in us from waking up until going to sleep. We will feel how this capricious element in our inner life can only be compared with the way things happen in the earth's atmosphere. And the principle which governs our thinking, feeling and doing is indeed like the earth's atmosphere. Our soul has the same powers in it, though only in embryonic form, as those that prevail in air and weather and in the elemental forces outside. These are the powers in us that govern thinking, feeling and doing. Out there they are elemental forces, demonic powers that live in air, water and fire, and in the thunder and lightning, the changeable weather conditions we have in the atmosphere around us. In our thinking, feeling and doing we are basically merely related to the activities which the earth develops out of its own egotism in winter. And people have been aware of this at all times.

---

[*] Alternative translation: thinking feeling and will.

When winter came and the earth's egotism with its elemental forces gained in influence, with the elemental forces now not following the sun, which they do in spring and summer, people felt that all this had a relationship with man's own inner life. Oh wintertime—people would feel though they would not express it clearly—you are related to my own inner life. But when the deep winter night came, the time of the winter solstice, people sensed that the sun was now gaining in power again, to be able to grow and grow and grow in strength towards spring and summer, and they felt: The sun's power always gains the victory over the earth's egotism. They would then feel courage and hope rising within them and were able to say: Just as in the physical world the cosmic sun always gains the upper hand over the terrestrial forces of the earth, as the victorious sun always irrupts into the dark winter night, if we just feel this, so there has to be something within the human being which reigns as spiritual sun in the depths of the soul. That spiritual sun will come and gain the victory—just as the year's sun gains victory in the winter solstice—and it will be the sun of the spirit in the great winter solstice to come. People first hoped and then knew that the time of the great winter solstice had come when they came to see the time of the Mystery on Golgotha as the rising of the spiritual sun in the inner life of human beings.

Let us now look at those early times in Earth evolution when it was the earth's spring and summer, before the Mystery on Golgotha. Human beings still had that inheritance from earlier times in them, the clairvoyance that made it possible for them to have vision in the spiritual world and they were still aware of their connection with the divine and spiritual world. Now, however, we are in earth's wintertime, something we cannot deny, a time when it has truly happened that we will not only be surrounded by mechanical forces to an increasing degree, forces that take effect in machines, in industry, in the commercial sphere of earthly activities, but we also live in such a way that we no longer have the divine and spiritual world around us the way it was in the time of earth's spring and summer. But the sun's victory at the time of the winter solstice, which in the past was felt to be symbolic, is something of which we may be sentient deep down in the human soul today as the victory of the spiritual sun when we contemplate the Mystery on Golgotha and the time of preparation for it when the child was born whose birth we celebrate anew at Christmas every year. Human beings need never doubt the power of the sun as winter approaches, they may indeed hope that the joys which autumn has taken from them will come again after the deep winter's night. And in the same way human beings may look to the events that happened in connection with the Mystery on Golgotha and say to themselves: The egotism of the human winter night may prevail, unruly and without order, as the gales do in winter nights, yet the hope will always remain that compared to the capriciousness in our own soul the Christ impulse which from the Mystery on Golgotha onwards has been connected with all human life on earth must win through. This is the Christ impulse which came into Earth evolution through the body of the Nathan Jesus child, and was able to come because the child of man who was born in that Nathan child, the child who had the qualities that belonged to the human soul when it had not yet gone through incarnations on earth, qualities in which the things connected with entry into incarnation on earth had not yet been implanted. That child still had the qualities of the highest of the spirit where it belongs for all eternity.

I wanted to present these ideas to you so that we may see how with regard to the childhood powers of man, which are also man's powers of development, human beings may be sentient of something most sublime, something people have always felt and shall continue to feel on beholding the divine infant on Holy Night. Our powers of insight must change, and in place of the things medieval minds saw in images we must gain different ideas—the idea of the two Jesus children, the inner nature of the one moving into the other, the Christ spirit taking possession of the Nathan Jesus child's body—but one thing remains and that is that we can look with our most sacred feelings and our greatest hopes to the insight that tells us: From the Mystery on Golgotha onwards, something has lived in the development of our humanity that has entered into the aura of our earth, and we merely need to appeal to this in our joyful festivities as our hope in the imperishable nature of our essential human nature.

It is just as necessary for us to be reminded of this as it was for the people who in the past took pleasure in watching those simple plays.

Indeed we may also say that we take just as much pleasure in seeing the plays. We feel connected with those people of the past because we know how to appreciate in our own way what was given to humanity when the child of man entered into Earth evolution. They were given the greatest hope, the greatest impulse which humanity needs so that in earth's wintertime, in the time after the Mystery on Golgotha, they may stay strong by beholding the sun in the physical cosmos gaining the upper hand over earth's egotism. More and more the impulses will live in the depths of the human soul that came through the Mystery on Golgotha as the spiritual sun impulse entering into human evolution on earth. The event came once in history by which this impulse entered into life on earth, but it needs to grow up again and again as it is remembered, which is what can happen with such festivals. You see, on the one hand it is true that the Christ spirit once entered into the earth's aura through the Mystery on Golgotha, and on the other hand it is true what Angelus Silesius[51] put into such beautiful words:

> The Christ could be born a thousand times in Bethlehem—
> but all in vain lest he is born in me.

The element that was born in Bethlehem must be born deep down and ever deeper in our own soul so that we see fulfilled for this soul of ours what medieval feeling wanted to see fulfilled when people saw the destiny of souls that were filled with the Christ impulse in those childlike figures which the angels took up to the Elysian Fields, figures that did not fall into the claws of Ahriman; only souls that had connected so much with earthly life that they seemed old would do so, though it is the destiny of souls not to grow old on earth but remain young. It is the body's destiny on earth to grow old. It is man's higher destiny to maintain a young mind in an ageing body in connection with the Mystery on Golgotha and so feel ever increasing hope that, however much winter's gales may rage in the soul and temptations may live in the soul, the living trust shall never end that the element that entered into the earth's aura through the Mystery on Golgotha shall rise from the depths of the soul. This is what we want to bring alive again in our souls with festivals like these.

I have tried, therefore, to bring together exactly what we are able to know as the Christmas mood, seeking to bring together in these few words what we feel in relation to Christmas, taking the anthroposophical point of view, and the experience people had in earlier times with the tidings of the divine infant when they saw a play like the one we have been performing.[52] It may be expressed in the following words:

Deep down in the human soul
Lives the sun of the spirit,
Certain of victory;
Powers of the true heart and mind sense it
In the winter of our inner life,
Sense the new shoot of hope in our heart;
Sun spirit's victory
Is what we behold
In blessed Christmas light,
Symbol of life most sublime
In winter's deepest night.

LECTURE 10

LEIPZIG, 12 JANUARY 1913

O UR life has to show, as it were, what we can be thanks to anthroposophy. This needs an open eye for life and sound judgement concerning it. Life is more complicated in our time than it was in earlier times. Not all that long ago it was much less complicated. That was because circumstances were less complex. In those days soulfulness and the qualities connected with it were still more widespread. Many other things have also changed. And we are all of us part of this changed life and we must try to penetrate the sphere of life in which we are to the necessary extent. It is very important exactly in present-day life that in spite of the fragmentation of modern life we find harmony in the soul and an inner cohesion in heart and mind.

This cannot be exhaustively covered in a lecture; all we can do is speak of details. Today we see materialism everywhere, including a materialism brought about by the use of machines that is present throughout practical life. This has made business life as well as life in general much more complex, has led to people being caught up in the hustle and bustle so that they have no time to reflect. People often do not even realize that all their energy, all their thinking from morning till night, is devoted to meeting material needs. So it is natural for people to think in a materialistic way in an age when the noise of engines is all around them. In a different age it would have been quite impossible for a materialistic and monistic philosophy of life to be so widespread.

We anthroposophists have a new philosophy of life. The spiritual movement goes out into the world. Consider the difficulties we meet with, consider how small the movement has remained in spite of its magnificent potential. Let us compare with this how religious confessions reign in the world outside, a relic from past ages. We find there all kinds of religious endeavours. We should take a good look at these. We find that religion is taken very intellectually. There are preachers, Christian preachers, who no longer believe in a human Christ, nor in immortality. People are glad when a Jatho movement[53] and the like comes up and is presented in as rationalistic a way as possible. All the old authorities cannot compete with blind faith in things that are scientifically established. These phenomena are all connected with moral attitudes. Business people will agree with me that there is little room for the truth in the dealings between seller and buyer today. People with a sense of responsibility suffer from this. Do the cobweb-thin concepts of such rational preachers have moral powers in them? Public opinion, of which people are so proud today, also did not exist in the thirteenth and fourteenth centuries the way it does today thanks to the daily papers. Great philosophers have long since said that public opinion consists in private misconceptions.[54] Could anyone make an Ostwald[55] believe that spiritual entities are connected with him? Yet by denying them he calls up specific spiritual entities. A host of quite specific spirits trails behind an Ostwald. The spirit lives in all matter. There is a spirit that is particularly interested in denying its spirit, and that is Ahriman. If people concentrate only on material laws, they will not drive the spirits away but conjure them up. They creep into the brains of materialists. Mephistopheles[56] sent Faust to the Mothers, saying: 'You will find a void there.' Faust's answer was, 'I hope to see your Nothing turn to Everything for me.' But the people of today do not give Faust's answer, for they are materialists possessed by Ahriman.

A different spirit is active in rationalistic religious thinking—Lucifer. With abstract notions, flimsy as cobwebs, he takes people away from the truly spiritual. Ideas are now said to live in history, which is as clever as saying that a painter who is himself but a painting is supposed to produce paintings. Being thus caught up in matter was in preparation for a long time. Today it has come to a temporary peak. Heraclitus[57] diluted theosophy into philosophy under the influence of Lucifer. This is reflected in his saying that he offered his book as a sacrifice to Artemis, at her temple in Ephesus.

Let us now consider public opinion. It arises from a law which is that Lucifer and Ahriman had to intervene in the image of the world. Before public opinion existed there were people whose inner life extended so far that it reached the spiritual secrets. They would have a good or bad influence on life in the world. We understand this if we study the history of Florence, for instance, from 1100 to 1500. Today we have people instead who endeavour to make a connection with the spiritual sphere. However, the luciferic spirits that remained behind on the moon did not reach this point, and it is they who determine public opinion. The result is that it lags about a thousand years behind. It is the lowliest among those spirits who work on public opinion, the recruits, we might say, in the luciferic army. They develop and will at a later time be powerful spirits. They are sitting behind the editorial desk, standing behind popular speakers, and so on. They are luciferic spirits taking their first steps in the art, mere nippers as yet.

To know one's way around in life is part of practical spiritual science. People use the rational mind to form their own picture of the world. What does this insight using rational mind and senses lead to? There is an old saying. Not even the representatives called to do so are able to grasp it. The serpent says, 'You shall be as gods, knowing good and evil.'[58] All insight based on intellect and senses is luciferic, is Lucifer's true sign and symbol. Insisting that only external experience counts where nothing counts but atoms—those are fantasies. It is not atoms which are behind the Maya but the spiritual realities. All phenomena people describe there are not real; it is the spiritual entities which are real. Monads[59] do not exist unless we take them in their reality as the higher hierarchies. There are many hierarchies, with the divinities of the Trinity among the highest of them. Philosophy refers to just one single whole. Yet there are many spirits, and the single whole exists only in the souls of the spirits. Anyone who has got used to thinking in such a way that he knows himself to be within the community of spirits knows the moral laws. Ahriman lets human beings be lost in the swamp of matter; Lucifer distracts them from the truth, not letting them sense that they are lost in a world that is all illusion. Maya has its justification if it is seen as a reflection of the reality that lies behind it.

NOTES

Origin of text material: The lectures given in 1913/14 have been published in Nos 150, 152 and 154 of the collected works in German (bibliography of 1961). Those on the subject of stages preceding the Mystery on Golgotha appeared in one volume. The rest, with some additional ones from the same period, have been published in two volumes (150 and 154). Volume 154 has appeared in English under the title *The Presence of the Dead on the Spiritual Path* (tr. C. von Arnim).

The notes may be considered good on the whole, except for inadequacies in the records of the lectures given on 13 April 1913 (morning and evening) and the lecture given on 5 May 1913, which cannot be said to be a true record of Rudolf Steiner's words in all parts. The limited notes on the lecture given on 12 January 1913 have been put at the end of this volume.

1. Rudolf Steiner, *The Education of the Child*, essay, tr. M. & G. Adams, Rudolf Steiner Press, London 1981.

2. The German writer Jean Paul Friedrich Richter (1763–1825): 'I'll never forget something I have never told before of the birth of my self-awareness, where I remember both place and time. It was a very young child, standing at the front door one morning. I was looking at the woodpile which was to the left. Suddenly the inner vision "I am an I" came before me like a flash of lightning from above and never left me. My I had seen itself for the first time and for ever. It is unlikely that memory deceives, for no one told me of this event which happened in a human being's veiled holy of holies, its newness alone making the everyday circumstances around me memorable.' From *Wahrheit aus Jean Pauls Leben*, Breslau 1826–8, No. 1, p. 53. Autobiography in form of a series of lectures. Published in Munich in 1970 under the title *Selbst-erlebensbeschreibung* in the writer's collected works, edited by Norbert Miller, vol. 6.

3. See Note 1.

4. See Scene 6 in Rudolf Steiner's *The Guardian of the Threshold*.

5. Munich, 10 March 1913.

6. Auerbach's Tavern. Goethe, *Faust I*, tr. by David Luke, Oxford University Press, 1987.

7. See the chapter on the Guardian of the Threshold in Rudolf Steiner's *Knowledge of the/How to Know Higher Worlds*.

8. Founder of Zoroastrianism. See reference also in Rudolf Steiner's *Occult Science*.

9. The following note appears at the end of the lecture (? Question and Answer session).

    Physical body of the Christ is the sun

etheric body of the Christ the seven planets
astral body of the Christ the twelve signs of the zodiac
The I of the Christ is still far off.

10. See e.g. Rudolf Steiner's *The Spiritual Guidance of Man and Humanity*, and his lectures on St Luke's Gospel.

11. There is a problem with the notes. Considering the meaning it should probably be '... but it is not for me to assume responsibility'.

12. See the lecture given in Berlin on 24 December 1912 in R. Steiner's *The Festivals of the Seasons*.

13. Raphael (1483–1520).

14. Friedrich von Hardenberg, known as Novalis (1772–1801).

15. Gotthold Ephraim Lessing (1729–81). His actual words were, 'Or do you think ... that Raphael would not have been the greatest genius as a painter if he had been unfortunate enough to be born without hands?' *Emilia Galotti*, Act I, Scene 4.

16. In the Eunike family. See Rudolf Steiner, *An Autobiography*.

17. See Rudolf Steiner, *Practical Training in Thinking*, lecture given in Karlsruhe, 18 January 1909.

18. E.g. Berlin, 2 May 1912, in *Earthly and Cosmic Man*; Berlin, 5 May 1909, typescript Z147 at Rudolf Steiner House Library, London; Duesseldorf, 27 April 1913 in *Life between Death and Rebirth*; Dornach, 1 November 1916, typescript R 11 at Rudolf Steiner House Library.

19. Plato (427–347 BC).

20. Aristotle (384–322 BC).

21. Acts of the Apostles 17:15–34.

22. Acts of the Apostles, 9:3–6.

23. Speech centre in third left gyrus of the cerebrum. Named after Paul Broca (1824–80), French anthropologist and surgeon.

24. See e.g. Carl Vogt (1817–95), philosopher, actual words: '... that thoughts relate to the brain approximately as the bile to the liver ...', in *Physiologische Briefe an die Gebildeten aller Stände*, Stuttgart and Tübingen 1845, p. 26.

25. Imperial Palace, Throne Room, 4900. Goethe, *Faust II*, tr. David Luke, Oxford University Press, 1994.

26. Goethe in a letter to Chancellor von Müller dated 24 May 1828. Actual words: 'Yet since matter never exists or can be effective without spirit, nor spirit without matter, matter is able to enhance itself, just as the spirit insists on its right to attract and repel.' Ph. Stein, *Goethe-Briefe*, Berlin 1924, vol. 8, p. 251.

27. Johannes Kepler (1571–1630), astronomer.

28. Giordano Bruno (1548–1600), Italian philosopher, co-founder of modern philosophy of life, burned at the stake by the Inquisition.

29. See Rudolf Steiner, *Occult Science, an Outline*.

30. Blaise Pascal (1623–62), French mathematician and philosopher.

31. In Fragment 72 in *Über die Religion und über einige andere Gegenstände* (on religion and some other subjects), 7th edn, Heidelberg 1972, p. 43.

32. Maurice Maeterlinck (1862–1949), Belgian writer.

33. Lecture given in Stockholm on 9 June 1913 on the subject of recognizing and

experiencing immortality in the light of anthroposophical insight (no record survives).

34. Sir William Crookes (1832–1919), British physicist and chemist. Among other things discovered thallium.

35. Another version says: 'in his studies with his medium'.

36. See Note 33.

37. See Note 23.

38. Genesis 3:5.

39. John 10:34.

40. Exclusion from the Theosophical Society and the establishment of the Anthroposophical Society. The exclusion was announced in a letter that Annie Besant wrote to Rudolf Steiner on 7 March 1913, informing him of the decision to dissolve the German Section. The Anthroposophical Society had been established on 2/3 February 1913.

41. See Note 10.

42. See *The Childhood of Jesus: The Unknown Years* by Emil Bock.

43. In *Cherubinic Wandersmann* (Cherubinic wanderer) 2657, book 1, verse 61.

44. The lecture had been preceded by a performance of the Oberufer *Three Kings' Play*.

45. See Note 10.

46. See Note 42.

47. Galileo Galilei (1564–1642), Italian physicist. Known as the father of modern science.

48. See Rudolf Steiner, 1st lecture in *Kunstgeschichte als Abbild innerer geistiger Impulse* (German collected works No. 292). Translated but not yet published [Anthroposophic Press].

49. See Rudolf Steiner, *The Spiritual Guidance of Man and Humanity*.

50. Giotto (1266–1337), Italian painter.

51. Angelus Silesius, see Note 43.

52. See Note 44.

53. Karl Jatho (1851–1913), Protestant cleric in Germany who was removed from office for his free-thinking ways.

54. Has not been traced so far. May be the words of Friedrich Nietzsche in 'Public opinions—private laziness', aphorism No. 482 in *Human, All too Human*.

55. Wilhelm Ostwald (1853–1932), German chemist. Founder of energetic philosophy of life.

56. Goethe, *Faust II*, Dark Gallery. David Luke translation.

57. Heraclitus (*c.* 545–480 BC), Greek philosopher.

58. Genesis 3:5.

59. Philosophical term meaning 'unit' (Leibniz).

RUDOLF STEINER'S COLLECTED WORKS

The German Edition of Rudolf Steiner's Collected Works (the *Gesamtausgabe* [GA] published by Rudolf Steiner Verlag, Dornach, Switzerland) presently runs to 354 titles, organized either by type of work (written or spoken), chronology, audience (public or other), or subject (education, art, etc.). For ease of comparison, the Collected Works in English [CW] follows the German organization exactly. A complete listing of the CWs follows with literal translations of the German titles. Other than in the case of the books published in his lifetime, titles were rarely given by Rudolf Steiner himself, and were often provided by the editors of the German editions. The titles in English are not necessarily the same as the German; and, indeed, over the past seventy-five years have frequently been different, with the same book sometimes appearing under different titles.

For ease of identification and to avoid confusion, we suggest that readers looking for a title should do so by CW number. Because the work of creating the Collected Works of Rudolf Steiner is an ongoing process, with new titles being published every year, we have not indicated in this listing which books are presently available. To find out what titles in the Collected Works are currently in print, please check our website at www.rudolfsteinerpress.com (or www.steinerbooks.org for US readers).

Written Work

CW 1	Goethe: Natural-Scientific Writings, Introduction, with Footnotes and Explanations in the text by Rudolf Steiner
CW 2	Outlines of an Epistemology of the Goethean World View, with Special Consideration of Schiller
CW 3	Truth and Science
CW 4	The Philosophy of Freedom
CW 4a	Documents to 'The Philosophy of Freedom'
CW 5	Friedrich Nietzsche, A Fighter against His Time
CW 6	Goethe's Worldview
CW 6a	Now in CW 30
CW 7	Mysticism at the Dawn of Modern Spiritual Life and Its Relationship with Modern Worldviews
CW 8	Christianity as Mystical Fact and the Mysteries of Antiquity
CW 9	Theosophy: An Introduction into Supersensible World Knowledge and Human Purpose
CW 10	How Does One Attain Knowledge of Higher Worlds?
CW 11	From the Akasha-Chronicle

Public Lectures

Lectures to the Members of the Anthroposophical Society

SIGNIFICANT EVENTS IN THE LIFE OF RUDOLF STEINER

1829:   June 23: birth of Johann Steiner (1829–1910)—Rudolf Steiner's father—in Geras, Lower Austria.

1834:   May 8: birth of Franciska Blie (1834–1918)—Rudolf Steiner's mother—in Horn, Lower Austria. 'My father and mother were both children of the glorious Lower Austrian forest district north of the Danube.'

1860:   May 16: marriage of Johann Steiner and Franciska Blie.

1861:   February 25: birth of *Rudolf Joseph Lorenz Steiner* in Kraljevec, Croatia, near the border with Hungary, where Johann Steiner works as a telegrapher for the South Austria Railroad. Rudolf Steiner is baptized two days later, February 27, the date usually given as his birthday.

1862:   Summer: the family moves to Mödling, Lower Austria.

1863:   The family moves to Pottschach, Lower Austria, near the Styrian border, where Johann Steiner becomes stationmaster. 'The view stretched to the mountains ... majestic peaks in the distance and the sweet charm of nature in the immediate surroundings.'

1864:   November 15: birth of Rudolf Steiner's sister, Leopoldine (d. November 1, 1927). She will become a seamstress and live with her parents for the rest of her life.

1866:   July 28: birth of Rudolf Steiner's deaf-mute brother, Gustav (d. May 1, 1941).

1867:   Rudolf Steiner enters the village school. Following a disagreement between his father and the schoolmaster, whose wife falsely accused the boy of causing a commotion, Rudolf Steiner is taken out of school and taught at home.

1868:   A critical experience. Unknown to the family, an aunt dies in a distant town. Sitting in the station waiting room, Rudolf Steiner sees her 'form,' which speaks to him, asking for help. 'Beginning with this experience, a new soul life began in the boy, one in which not only the outer trees and mountains spoke to him, but also the worlds that lay behind them. From this moment on, the boy began to live with the spirits of nature...'

1869:   The family moves to the peaceful, rural village of Neudörfl, near Wiener-Neustadt in present-day Austria. Rudolf Steiner attends the village school. Because of the 'unorthodoxy' of his writing and spelling, he has to do 'extra lessons'.

1870:   Through a book lent to him by his tutor, he discovers geometry: 'To grasp something purely in the spirit brought me inner happiness. I know that I first learned happiness through geometry.' The same tutor allows him to draw, while other students still struggle with their reading and writing. 'An artistic element' thus enters his education.

1871:   Though his parents are not religious, Rudolf Steiner becomes a 'church child,' a favourite of the priest, who was 'an exceptional character'. 'Up to the age of ten or eleven, among those I came to know, he was far and away the most significant.' Among other things, he introduces Steiner to Copernican, heliocentric cosmology. As an altar boy, Rudolf Steiner serves at Masses, funerals, and Corpus Christi processions. At year's end, after an incident in which he escapes a thrashing, his father forbids him to go to church.

1872:   Rudolf Steiner transfers to grammar school in Wiener-Neustadt, a five-mile walk from home, which must be done in all weathers.

1873–75: Through his teachers and on his own, Rudolf Steiner has many wonderful experiences with science and mathematics. Outside school, he teaches himself analytic geometry, trigonometry, differential equations, and calculus.

1876:   Rudolf Steiner begins tutoring other students. He learns bookbinding from his father. He also teaches himself stenography.

1877:   Rudolf Steiner discovers Kant's *Critique of Pure Reason*, which he reads and rereads. He also discovers and reads von Rotteck's *World History*.

1878:   He studies extensively in contemporary psychology and philosophy.

1879:   Rudolf Steiner graduates from high school with honours. His father is transferred to Inzersdorf, near Vienna. He uses his first visit to Vienna 'to purchase a great number of philosophy books'—Kant, Fichte, Schelling, and Hegel, as well as numerous histories of philosophy. His aim: to find a path from the 'I' to nature.

October 1879–1883: Rudolf Steiner attends the Technical College in Vienna—to study mathematics, chemistry, physics, mineralogy, botany, zoology, biology, geology, and mechanics—with a scholarship. He also attends lectures in history and literature, while avidly reading philosophy on his own. His two favourite professors are Karl Julius Schröer (German language and literature) and Edmund Reitlinger (physics). He also audits lectures by Robert Zimmerman on aesthetics and Franz Brentano on philosophy. During this year he begins his friendship with Moritz Zitter (1861–1921), who will help support him financially when he is in Berlin.

1880:   Rudolf Steiner attends lectures on Schiller and Goethe by Karl Julius Schröer, who becomes his mentor. Also 'through a remarkable combination of circumstances,' he meets Felix Koguzki, a 'herb gatherer' and healer, who could 'see deeply into the secrets of nature'. Rudolf Steiner will meet and study with this 'emissary of the Master' throughout his time in Vienna.

1881:   January: '... I didn't sleep a wink. I was busy with philosophical problems until about 12:30 a.m. Then, finally, I threw myself down on my couch. All my striving during the previous year had been to research whether the following statement by Schelling was true or not: *Within everyone dwells a secret, marvelous capacity to draw back from the stream of time—out of the self clothed in all that comes to us from outside—into our innermost being and there, in the immutable form of the Eternal, to look into ourselves*. I believe, and I am still quite certain of it, that I discovered this capacity in myself; I had long had an inkling of it. Now the whole of idealist philosophy stood before me in modified form. What's a sleepless night compared to that!'

Rudolf Steiner begins communicating with leading thinkers of the day, who send him books in return, which he reads eagerly.

July: 'I am not one of those who dives into the day like an animal in human form. I pursue a quite specific goal, an idealistic aim—knowledge of the truth! This cannot be done offhandedly. It requires the greatest striving in the world, free of all egotism, and equally of all resignation.'

August: Steiner puts down on paper for the first time thoughts for a 'Philosophy of Freedom.' 'The striving for the absolute: this human yearning is freedom.' He also seeks to outline a 'peasant philosophy,' describing what the worldview of a 'peasant'—one who lives close to the earth and the old ways—really is.

1881–1882: Felix Koguzki, the herb gatherer, reveals himself to be the envoy of another, higher initiatory personality, who instructs Rudolf Steiner to penetrate Fichte's philosophy and to master modern scientific thinking as a preparation for right entry into the spirit. This 'Master' also teaches him the double (evolutionary and involutionary) nature of time.

1882:   Through the offices of Karl Julius Schröer, Rudolf Steiner is asked by Joseph Kurschner to edit Goethe's scientific works for the *Deutschen National-Literatur* edition. He writes 'A Possible Critique of Atomistic Concepts' and sends it to Friedrich Theodore Vischer.

1883:   Rudolf Steiner completes his college studies and begins work on the Goethe project.

1884:   First volume of Goethe's *Scientific Writings* (CW 1) appears (March). He lectures on Goethe and Lessing, and Goethe's approach to science. In July, he enters the household of Ladislaus and Pauline Specht as tutor to the four Specht boys. He will live there until 1890. At this time, he meets Josef Breuer (1842–1925), the co-author with Sigmund Freud of *Studies in Hysteria*, who is the Specht family doctor.

1885:   While continuing to edit Goethe's writings, Rudolf Steiner reads deeply in contemporary philosophy (Edouard von Hartmann, Johannes Volkelt, and Richard Wahle, among others).

1886:   May: Rudolf Steiner sends Kurschner the manuscript of *Outlines of Goethe's Theory of Knowledge* (CW 2), which appears in October, and which he sends out widely. He also meets the poet Marie Eugenie Delle Grazie and writes 'Nature and Our Ideals' for her. He attends her salon, where he meets many priests, theologians, and philosophers, who will become his friends. Meanwhile, the director of the Goethe Archive in Weimar requests his collaboration with the *Sophien* edition of Goethe's works, particularly the writings on colour.

1887:   At the beginning of the year, Rudolf Steiner is very sick. As the year progresses and his health improves, he becomes increasingly 'a man of letters,' lecturing, writing essays, and taking part in Austrian cultural life. In August–September, the second volume of Goethe's *Scientific Writings* appears.

1888: January–July: Rudolf Steiner assumes editorship of the 'German Weekly' (*Deutsche Wochenschrift*). He begins lecturing more intensively, giving, for example, a lecture titled 'Goethe as Father of a New Aesthetics.' He meets and becomes soul friends with Friedrich Eckstein (1861–1939), a vegetarian, philosopher of symbolism, alchemist, and musician, who will introduce him to various spiritual currents (including Theosophy) and with whom he will meditate and interpret esoteric and alchemical texts.

1889: Rudolf Steiner first reads Nietzsche (*Beyond Good and Evil*). He encounters Theosophy again and learns of Madame Blavatsky in the Theosophical circle around Marie Lang (1858–1934). Here he also meets well-known figures of Austrian life, as well as esoteric figures like the occultist Franz Hartmann and Karl Leinigen-Billigen (translator of C.G. Harrison's *The Transcendental Universe*). During this period, Steiner first reads A.P. Sinnett's *Esoteric Buddhism* and Mabel Collins's *Light on the Path*. He also begins travelling, visiting Budapest, Weimar, and Berlin (where he meets philosopher Edouard von Hartmann).

1890: Rudolf Steiner finishes volume 3 of Goethe's scientific writings. He begins his doctoral dissertation, which will become *Truth and Science* (CW 3). He also meets the poet and feminist Rosa Mayreder (1858–1938), with whom he can exchange his most intimate thoughts. In September, Rudolf Steiner moves to Weimar to work in the Goethe-Schiller Archive.

1891: Volume 3 of the Kurschner edition of Goethe appears. Meanwhile, Rudolf Steiner edits Goethe's studies in mineralogy and scientific writings for the *Sophien* edition. He meets Ludwig Laistner of the Cotta Publishing Company, who asks for a book on the basic question of metaphysics. From this will result, ultimately, *The Philosophy of Freedom* (CW 4), which will be published not by Cotta but by Emil Felber. In October, Rudolf Steiner takes the oral exam for a doctorate in philosophy, mathematics, and mechanics at Rostock University, receiving his doctorate on the twenty-sixth. In November, he gives his first lecture on Goethe's 'Fairy Tale' in Vienna.

1892: Rudolf Steiner continues work at the Goethe-Schiller Archive and on his *Philosophy of Freedom*. *Truth and Science*, his doctoral dissertation, is published. Steiner undertakes to write introductions to books on Schopenhauer and Jean Paul for Cotta. At year's end, he finds lodging with Anna Eunike, née Schulz (1853–1911), a widow with four daughters and a son. He also develops a friendship with Otto Erich Hartleben (1864–1905) with whom he shares literary interests.

1893: Rudolf Steiner begins his habit of producing many reviews and articles. In March, he gives a lecture titled 'Hypnotism, with Reference to Spiritism.' In September, volume 4 of the Kurschner edition is completed. In November, *The Philosophy of Freedom* appears. This year, too, he meets John Henry Mackay (1864–1933), the anarchist, and Max Stirner, a scholar and biographer.

1894: Rudolf Steiner meets Elisabeth Förster Nietzsche, the philosopher's sister, and begins to read Nietzsche in earnest, beginning with the as yet unpublished *Antichrist*. He also meets Ernst Haeckel (1834–1919). In the fall, he begins to write *Nietzsche, A Fighter against His Time* (CW 5).

1895: May, *Nietzsche, A Fighter against His Time* appears.

1896: January 22: Rudolf Steiner sees Friedrich Nietzsche for the first and only time. Moves between the Nietzsche and the Goethe-Schiller Archives, where he completes his work before year's end. He falls out with Elisabeth Förster Nietzsche, thus ending his association with the Nietzsche Archive.

1897: Rudolf Steiner finishes the manuscript of *Goethe's Worldview* (CW 6). He moves to Berlin with Anna Eunike and begins editorship of the *Magazin für Literatur*. From now on, Steiner will write countless reviews, literary and philosophical articles, and so on. He begins lecturing at the 'Free Literary Society.' In September, he attends the Zionist Congress in Basel. He sides with Dreyfus in the Dreyfus affair.

1898: Rudolf Steiner is very active as an editor in the political, artistic, and theatrical life of Berlin. He becomes friendly with John Henry Mackay and poet Ludwig Jacobowski (1868–1900). He joins Jacobowski's circle of writers, artists, and scientists—'The Coming Ones' (*Die Kommenden*)—and contributes lectures to the group until 1903. He also lectures at the 'League for College Pedagogy.' He writes an article for Goethe's sesquicentennial, 'Goethe's Secret Revelation,' on the 'Fairy Tale of the Green Snake and the Beautiful Lily.'

1898–99: 'This was a trying time for my soul as I looked at Christianity. . . . I was able to progress only by contemplating, by means of spiritual perception, the evolution of Christianity. . . . Conscious knowledge of real Christianity began to dawn in me around the turn of the century. This seed continued to develop. My soul trial occurred shortly before the beginning of the twentieth century. It was decisive for my soul's development that I stood spiritually before the Mystery of Golgotha in a deep and solemn celebration of knowledge.'

1899: Rudolf Steiner begins teaching and giving lectures and lecture cycles at the Workers' College, founded by Wilhelm Liebknecht (1826–1900). He will continue to do so until 1904. Writes: *Literature and Spiritual Life in the Nineteenth Century; Individualism in Philosophy; Haeckel and His Opponents; Poetry in the Present;* and begins what will become (fifteen years later) *The Riddles of Philosophy* (CW 18). He also meets many artists and writers, including Käthe Kollwitz, Stefan Zweig, and Rainer Maria Rilke. On October 31, he marries Anna Eunike.

1900: 'I thought that the turn of the century must bring humanity a new light. It seemed to me that the separation of human thinking and willing from the spirit had peaked. A turn or reversal of direction in human evolution seemed to me a necessity.' Rudolf Steiner finishes *World and Life Views in the Nineteenth Century* (the second part of what will become *The Riddles of Philosophy*) and dedicates it to Ernst Haeckel. It is published in March. He continues lecturing at *Die Kommenden*, whose leadership he assumes after the death of Jacobowski. Also, he gives the Gutenberg Jubilee lecture before 7,000 typesetters and printers. In September, Rudolf Steiner is invited by Count and Countess Brockdorff to lecture in the Theosophical Library. His first lecture is on Nietzsche. His second lecture is titled 'Goethe's Secret Revelation.' October 6, he begins a lecture cycle on the mystics that will become *Mystics after Modernism* (CW 7). November-December: 'Marie von Sivers appears in the audience....' Also in November, Steiner gives his first lecture at the Giordano Bruno Bund (where he will continue to lecture until May, 1905). He speaks on Bruno and modern Rome, focusing on the importance of the philosophy of Thomas Aquinas as monism.

1901:   In continual financial straits, Rudolf Steiner's early friends Moritz Zitter and Rosa Mayreder help support him. In October, he begins the lecture cycle *Christianity as Mystical Fact* (CW 8) at the Theosophical Library. In November, he gives his first 'Theosophical lecture' on Goethe's 'Fairy Tale' in Hamburg at the invitation of Wilhelm Hubbe-Schleiden. He also attends a gathering to celebrate the founding of the Theosophical Society at Count and Countess Brockdorff's. He gives a lecture cycle, 'From Buddha to Christ,' for the circle of the *Kommenden*. November 17, Marie von Sivers asks Rudolf Steiner if Theosophy needs a Western-Christian spiritual movement (to complement Theosophy's Eastern emphasis). 'The question was posed. Now, following spiritual laws, I could begin to give an answer....' In December, Rudolf Steiner writes his first article for a Theosophical publication. At year's end, the Brockdorffs and possibly Wilhelm Hubbe-Schleiden ask Rudolf Steiner to join the Theosophical Society and undertake the leadership of the German section. Rudolf Steiner agrees, on the condition that Marie von Sivers (then in Italy) work with him.

1902:   Beginning in January, Rudolf Steiner attends the opening of the Workers' School in Spandau with Rosa Luxemburg (1870–1919). January 17, Rudolf Steiner joins the Theosophical Society. In April, he is asked to become general secretary of the German Section of the Theosophical Society, and works on preparations for its founding. In July, he visits London for a Theosophical congress. He meets Bertram Keightly, G.R.S. Mead, A.P. Sinnett, and Annie Besant, among others. In September, *Christianity as Mystical Fact* appears. In October, Rudolf Steiner gives his first public lecture on Theosophy ('Monism and Theosophy') to about three hundred people at the Giordano Bruno Bund. On October 19–21, the German Section of the Theosophical Society has its first meeting; Rudolf Steiner is the general secretary, and Annie Besant attends. Steiner lectures on practical karma studies. On October 23, Annie Besant inducts Rudolf Steiner into the Esoteric School of the Theosophical Society. On October 25, Steiner begins a weekly series of lectures: 'The Field of Theosophy.' During this year, Rudolf Steiner also first meets Ita Wegman (1876–1943), who will become his close collaborator in his final years.

1903:   Rudolf Steiner holds about 300 lectures and seminars. In May, the first issue of the periodical *Luzifer* appears. In June, Rudolf Steiner visits

London for the first meeting of the Federation of the European Sections of the Theosophical Society, where he meets Colonel Olcott. He begins to write *Theosophy* (CW 9).

1904: Rudolf Steiner continues lecturing at the Workers' College and elsewhere (about 90 lectures), while lecturing intensively all over Germany among Theosophists (about 140 lectures). In February, he meets Carl Unger (1878–1929), who will become a member of the board of the Anthroposophical Society (1913). In March, he meets Michael Bauer (1871–1929), a Christian mystic, who will also be on the board. In May, *Theosophy* appears, with the dedication: 'To the spirit of Giordano Bruno.' Rudolf Steiner and Marie von Sivers visit London for meetings with Annie Besant. June: Rudolf Steiner and Marie von Sivers attend the meeting of the Federation of European Sections of the Theosophical Society in Amsterdam. In July, Steiner begins the articles in *Luzifer-Gnosis* that will become *How to Know Higher Worlds* (CW 10) and *Cosmic Memory* (CW 11). In September, Annie Besant visits Germany. In December, Steiner lectures on Freemasonry. He mentions the High Grade Masonry derived from John Yarker and represented by Theodore Reuss and Karl Kellner as a blank slate 'into which a good image could be placed'.

1905: This year, Steiner ends his non-Theosophical lecturing activity. Supported by Marie von Sivers, his Theosophical lecturing—both in public and in the Theosophical Society—increases significantly: 'The German Theosophical Movement is of exceptional importance.' Steiner recommends reading, among others, Fichte, Jacob Boehme, and Angelus Silesius. He begins to introduce Christian themes into Theosophy. He also begins to work with doctors (Felix Peipers and Ludwig Noll). In July, he is in London for the Federation of European Sections, where he attends a lecture by Annie Besant: 'I have seldom seen Mrs. Besant speak in so inward and heartfelt a manner....' 'Through Mrs. Besant I have found the way to H.P. Blavatsky.' September to October, he gives a course of thirty-one lectures for a small group of esoteric students. In October, the annual meeting of the German Section of the Theosophical Society, which still remains very small, takes place. Rudolf Steiner reports membership has risen from 121 to 377 members. In November, seeking to establish esoteric 'continuity,' Rudolf Steiner and Marie von Sivers participate in a 'Memphis-Misraim' Masonic ceremony. They pay forty-five marks for membership. 'Yesterday, you saw how little remains of former esoteric institutions.' 'We are dealing only with a "framework"... for the present, nothing lies behind it. The occult powers have completely withdrawn.'

1906: Expansion of Theosophical work. Rudolf Steiner gives about 245 lectures, only 44 of which take place in Berlin. Cycles are given in Paris, Leipzig, Stuttgart, and Munich. Esoteric work also intensifies. Rudolf Steiner begins writing *An Outline of Esoteric Science* (CW 13). In January, Rudolf Steiner receives permission (a patent) from the Great Orient of the Scottish A & A Thirty-Three Degree Rite of the Order of the Ancient

Freemasons of the Memphis-Misraim Rite to direct a chapter under the name 'Mystica Aeterna.' This will become the 'Cognitive-Ritual Section' (also called 'Misraim Service') of the Esoteric School. (See: *Freemasonry and Ritual Work: The Misraim Service*, CW 265). During this time, Steiner also meets Albert Schweitzer. In May, he is in Paris, where he visits Edouard Schuré. Many Russians attend his lectures (including Konstantin Balmont, Dimitri Mereszkovski, Zinaida Hippius, and Maximilian Woloshin). He attends the General Meeting of the European Federation of the Theosophical Society, at which Col. Olcott is present for the last time. He spends the year's end in Venice and Rome, where he writes and works on his translation of H.P. Blavatsky's *Key to Theosophy*.

1907:   Further expansion of the German Theosophical Movement according to the Rosicrucian directive to 'introduce spirit into the world'—in education, in social questions, in art, and in science. In February, Col. Olcott dies in Adyar. Before he dies, Olcott indicates that 'the Masters' wish Annie Besant to succeed him: much politicking ensues. Rudolf Steiner supports Besant's candidacy. April-May: preparations for the Congress of the Federation of European Sections of the Theosophical Society—the great, watershed Whitsun 'Munich Congress,' attended by Annie Besant and others. Steiner decides to separate Eastern and Western (Christian-Rosicrucian) esoteric schools. He takes his esoteric school out of the Theosophical Society (Besant and Rudolf Steiner are 'in harmony' on this). Steiner makes his first lecture tours to Austria and Hungary. That summer, he is in Italy. In September, he visits Edouard Schuré, who will write the introduction to the French edition of *Christianity as Mystical Fact* in Barr, Alsace. Rudolf Steiner writes the autobiographical statement known as the 'Barr Document.' In *Luzifer-Gnosis*, 'The Education of the Child' appears.

1908:   The movement grows (membership: 1,150). Lecturing expands. Steiner makes his first extended lecture tour to Holland and Scandinavia, as well as visits to Naples and Sicily. Themes: St John's Gospel, the Apocalypse, Egypt, science, philosophy, and logic. *Luzifer-Gnosis* ceases publication. In Berlin, Marie von Sivers with Johanna Mücke (1864–1949) forms the *Philosophisch-Theosophisch* (after 1915 *Philosophisch-Anthroposophisch*) *Verlag* to publish Steiner's work. Steiner gives lecture cycles titled *The Gospel of St John* (CW 103) and *The Apocalypse* (104).

1909:   *An Outline of Esoteric Science* appears. Lecturing and travel continues. Rudolf Steiner's spiritual research expands to include the polarity of Lucifer and Ahriman; the work of great individualities in history; the Maitreya Buddha and the Bodhisattvas; spiritual economy (CW 109); the work of the spiritual hierarchies in heaven and on earth (CW 110). He also deepens and intensifies his research into the Gospels, giving lectures on the Gospel of St Luke (CW 114) with the first mention of two Jesus children. Meets and becomes friends with Christian Morgenstern (1871–1914). In April, he lays the foundation stone for the Malsch model—the building that will lead to the first Goetheanum. In May, the International Congress of the Federation of European Sections of the

Theosophical Society takes place in Budapest. Rudolf Steiner receives the Subba Row medal for *How to Know Higher Worlds*. During this time, Charles W. Leadbeater discovers Jiddu Krishnamurti (1895–1986) and proclaims him the future 'world teacher,' the bearer of the Maitreya Buddha and the 'reappearing Christ'. In October, Steiner delivers seminal lectures on 'anthroposophy,' which he will try, unsuccessfully, to rework over the next years into the unfinished work, *Anthroposophy (A Fragment)* (CW 45).

1910: New themes: *The Reappearance of Christ in the Etheric* (CW 118); *The Fifth Gospel; The Mission of Folk Souls* (CW 121); *Occult History* (CW 126); the evolving development of etheric cognitive capacities. Rudolf Steiner continues his Gospel research with *The Gospel of St Matthew* (CW 123). In January, his father dies. In April, he takes a month-long trip to Italy, including Rome, Monte Cassino, and Sicily. He also visits Scandinavia again. July–August, he writes the first mystery drama, *The Portal of Initiation* (CW 14). In November, he gives 'psychosophy' lectures. In December, he submits 'On the Psychological Foundations and Epistemological Framework of Theosophy' to the International Philosophical Congress in Bologna.

1911: The crisis in the Theosophical Society deepens. In January, 'The Order of the Rising Sun,' which will soon become 'The Order of the Star in the East,' is founded for the coming world teacher, Krishnamurti. At the same time, Marie von Sivers, Rudolf Steiner's co-worker, falls ill. Fewer lectures are given, but important new ground is broken. In Prague, in March, Steiner meets Franz Kafka (1883–1924) and Hugo Bergmann (1883-1975). In April, he delivers his paper to the Philosophical Congress. He writes the second mystery drama, *The Soul's Probation* (CW 14). Also, while Marie von Sivers is convalescing, Rudolf Steiner begins work on *Calendar 1912/1913*, which will contain the 'Calendar of the Soul' meditations. On March 19, Anna (Eunike) Steiner dies. In September, Rudolf Steiner visits Einsiedeln, birthplace of Paracelsus. In December, Friedrich Rittelmeyer, future founder of the Christian Community, meets Rudolf Steiner. The *Johannes-Bauverein*, the 'building committee,' which would lead to the first Goetheanum (first planned for Munich), is also founded, and a preliminary committee for the founding of an independent association is created that, in the following year, will become the Anthroposophical Society. Important lecture cycles include *Occult Physiology* (CW 128); *Wonders of the World* (CW 129); *From Jesus to Christ* (CW 131). Other themes: esoteric Christianity; Christian Rosenkreutz; the spiritual guidance of humanity; the sense world and the world of the spirit.

1912: Despite the ongoing, now increasing crisis in the Theosophical Society, much is accomplished: *Calendar 1912/1913* is published; eurythmy is created; both the third mystery drama, *The Guardian of the Threshold* (CW 14) and *A Way of Self-Knowledge* (CW 16) are written. New (or renewed) themes included life between death and rebirth and karma and reincarnation. Other lecture cycles: *Spiritual Beings in the Heavenly Bodies and in the Kingdoms of Nature* (CW 136); *The Human Being in the Light of Occultism, Theosophy, and Philosophy* (CW 137); *The Gospel of St Mark* (CW 139); and *The Bhagavad Gita and the Epistles of Paul* (CW 142). On May 8, Rudolf Steiner celebrates White Lotus Day, H.P. Blavatsky's death day, which he had faithfully observed for the past decade, for the last time. In August, Rudolf Steiner suggests the 'independent association' be called the 'Anthroposophical Society.' In September, the first eurythmy course takes place. In October, Rudolf Steiner declines recognition of a Theosophical Society lodge dedicated to the Star of the East and decides to expel all Theosophical Society members belonging to the order. Also, with Marie von Sivers, he first visits Dornach, near Basel, Switzerland, and they stand on the hill where the Goetheanum will be built. In November, a Theosophical Society lodge is opened by direct mandate from Adyar (Annie Besant). In December, a meeting of the German section occurs at which it is decided that belonging to the Order of the Star of the East is incompatible with membership in the Theosophical Society. December 28: informal founding of the Anthroposophical Society in Berlin.

1913: Expulsion of the German section from the Theosophical Society. February 2–3: Foundation meeting of the Anthroposophical Society. Board members include: Marie von Sivers, Michael Bauer, and Carl Unger. September 20: Laying of the foundation stone for the *Johannes Bau* (Goetheanum) in Dornach. Building begins immediately. The third mystery drama, *The Soul's Awakening* (CW 14), is completed. Also: *The Threshold of the Spiritual World* (CW 147). Lecture cycles include: *The Bhagavad Gita and the Epistles of Paul* and *The Esoteric Meaning of the Bhagavad Gita* (CW 146), which the Russian philosopher Nikolai Berdyaev attends; *The Mysteries of the East and of Christianity* (CW 144); *The Effects of Esoteric Development* (CW 145); and *The Fifth Gospel* (CW 148). In May, Rudolf Steiner is in London and Paris, where anthroposophical work continues.

1914: Building continues on the *Johannes Bau* (Goetheanum) in Dornach, with artists and co-workers from seventeen nations. The general assembly of the Anthroposophical Society takes place. In May, Rudolf Steiner visits Paris, as well as Chartres Cathedral. June 28: assassination in Sarajevo ('Now the catastrophe has happened!'). August 1: War is declared. Rudolf Steiner returns to Germany from Dornach—he will travel back and forth. He writes the last chapter of *The Riddles of Philosophy*. Lecture cycles include: *Human and Cosmic Thought* (CW 151); *Inner Being of Humanity between Death and a New Birth* (CW 153); *Occult Reading and Occult Hearing* (CW 156). December 24: marriage of Rudolf Steiner and Marie von Sivers.

1915: Building continues. Life after death becomes a major theme, also art. Writes: *Thoughts during a Time of War* (CW 24). Lectures include: *The Secret of Death* (CW 159); *The Uniting of Humanity through the Christ Impulse* (CW 165).

1916: Rudolf Steiner begins work with Edith Maryon (1872–1924) on the sculpture 'The Representative of Humanity' ('The Group'—Christ, Lucifer, and Ahriman). He also works with the alchemist Alexander von Bernus on the quarterly *Das Reich*. He writes *The Riddle of Humanity* (CW 20). Lectures include: *Necessity and Freedom in World History and Human Action* (CW 166); *Past and Present in the Human Spirit* (CW 167); *The Karma of Vocation* (CW 172); *The Karma of Untruthfulness* (CW 173).

1917: Russian Revolution. The U.S. enters the war. Building continues. Rudolf Steiner delineates the idea of the 'threefold nature of the human being' (in a public lecture March 15) and the 'threefold nature of the social organism' (hammered out in May-June with the help of Otto von Lerchenfeld and Ludwig Polzer-Hoditz in the form of two documents titled *Memoranda*, which were distributed in high places). August–September: Rudolf Steiner writes *The Riddles of the Soul* (CW 20). Also: commentary on 'The Chymical Wedding of Christian Rosenkreutz' for Alexander Bernus (*Das Reich*). Lectures include: *The Karma of Materialism* (CW 176); *The Spiritual Background of the Outer World: The Fall of the Spirits of Darkness* (CW 177).

1918: March 18: peace treaty of Brest-Litovsk—'Now everything will truly enter chaos! What is needed is cultural renewal.' June: Rudolf Steiner visits Karlstein (Grail) Castle outside Prague. Lecture cycle: *From Symptom to Reality in Modern History* (CW 185). In mid-November, Emil Molt, of the Waldorf-Astoria Cigarette Company, has the idea of founding a school for his workers' children.

1919: Focus on the threefold social organism: tireless travel, countless lectures, meetings, and publications. At the same time, a new public stage of Anthroposophy emerges as cultural renewal begins. The coming years will see initiatives in pedagogy, medicine, pharmacology, and agriculture. January 27: threefold meeting: ' We must first of all, with the money we have, found free schools that can bring people what they need.' February: first public eurythmy performance in Zurich. Also: 'Appeal to the German People' (CW 24), circulated March 6 as a newspaper insert. In April, *Towards Social Renewal* (CW 23) appears— 'perhaps the most widely read of all books on politics appearing since the war'. Rudolf Steiner is asked to undertake the 'direction and leadership' of the school founded by the Waldorf-Astoria Company. Rudolf Steiner begins to talk about the 'renewal' of education. May 30: a building is selected and purchased for the future Waldorf School. August–September, Rudolf Steiner gives a lecture course for Waldorf teachers, *The Foundations of Human Experience (Study of Man)* (CW 293). September 7: Opening of the first Waldorf School. December (into January): first science course, the *Light Course* (CW 320).

1920: The Waldorf School flourishes. New threefold initiatives. Founding of limited companies *Der Kommende Tag* and *Futurum A.G.* to infuse spiritual values into the economic realm. Rudolf Steiner also focuses on the sciences. Lectures: *Introducing Anthroposophical Medicine* (CW 312); *The Warmth Course* (CW 321); *The Boundaries of Natural Science* (CW 322); *The Redemption of Thinking* (CW 74). February: Johannes Werner

Klein—later a co-founder of the Christian Community—asks Rudolf Steiner about the possibility of a 'religious renewal,' a 'Johannine church'. In March, Rudolf Steiner gives the first course for doctors and medical students. In April, a divinity student asks Rudolf Steiner a second time about the possibility of religious renewal. September 27–October 16: anthroposophical 'university course'. December: lectures titled *The Search for the New Isis* (CW 202).

1921:   Rudolf Steiner continues his intensive work on cultural renewal, including the uphill battle for the threefold social order. 'University' arts, scientific, theological, and medical courses include: *The Astronomy Course* (CW 323); *Observation, Mathematics, and Scientific Experiment* (CW 324); the *Second Medical Course* (CW 313); *Colour*. In June and September-October, Rudolf Steiner also gives the first two 'priests' courses' (CW 342 and 343). The 'youth movement' gains momentum. Magazines are founded: *Die Drei* (January), and—under the editorship of Albert Steffen (1884–1963)—the weekly, *Das Goetheanum* (August). In February–March, Rudolf Steiner takes his first trip outside Germany since the war (Holland). On April 7, Steiner receives a letter regarding 'religious renewal,' and May 22–23, he agrees to address the question in a practical way. In June, the Klinical-Therapeutic Institute opens in Arlesheim under the direction of Dr Ita Wegman. In August, the Chemical-Pharmaceutical Laboratory opens in Arlesheim (Oskar Schmiedel and Ita Wegman are directors). The Clinical Therapeutic Institute is inaugurated in Stuttgart (Dr Ludwig Noll is director); also the Research Laboratory in Dornach (Ehrenfried Pfeiffer and Gunther Wachsmuth are directors). In November–December, Rudolf Steiner visits Norway.

1922:   The first half of the year involves very active public lecturing (thousands attend); in the second half, Rudolf Steiner begins to withdraw and turn toward the Society—'The Society is asleep.' It is 'too weak' to do what is asked of it. The businesses—*Der Kommende Tag* and *Futurum A.G.*—fail. In January, with the help of an agent, Steiner undertakes a twelve-city German lecture tour, accompanied by eurythmy performances. In two weeks he speaks to more than 2,000 people. In April, he gives a 'university course' in The Hague. He also visits England. In June, he is in Vienna for the East–West Congress. In August–September, he is back in England for the Oxford Conference on Education. Returning to Dornach, he gives the lectures *Philosophy, Cosmology, and Religion* (CW 215), and gives the third priests' course (CW 344). On September 16, The Christian Community is founded. In October–November, Steiner is in Holland and England. He also speaks to the youth: *The Youth Course* (CW 217). In December, Steiner gives lectures titled *The Origins of Natural Science* (CW 326), and *Humanity and the World of Stars: The Spiritual Communion of Humanity* (CW 219). December 31: Fire at the Goetheanum, which is destroyed.

1923:   Despite the fire, Rudolf Steiner continues his work unabated. A very hard year. Internal dispersion, dissension, and apathy abound. There is conflict—between old and new visions—within the Society. A wake-up call is needed, and Rudolf Steiner responds with renewed lecturing vitality. His focus: the spiritual context of human life; initiation science; the course of the year; and community building. As a foundation for an artistic school, he creates a series of pastel sketches. Lecture cycles: *The Anthroposophical Movement; Initiation Science* (CW 227) (in England at the Penmaenmawr Summer School); *The Four Seasons and the Archangels* (CW 229); *Harmony of the Creative Word* (CW 230); *The Supersensible Human* (CW 231), given in Holland for the founding of the Dutch society. On November 10, in response to the failed Hitler-Ludendorff putsch in Munich, Steiner closes his Berlin residence and moves the *Philosophisch-Anthroposophisch Verlag* (Press) to Dornach. On December 9, Steiner begins the serialization of his *Autobiography: The Course of My Life* (CW 28) in *Das Goetheanum*. It will continue to appear weekly, without a break, until his death. Late December–early January: Rudolf Steiner re-founds the Anthroposophical Society (about 12,000 members internationally) and takes over its leadership. The new board members are: Marie Steiner, Ita Wegman, Albert Steffen, Elizabeth Vreede, and Guenther Wachsmuth. (See *The Christmas Meeting for the Founding of the General Anthroposophical Society*, CW 260). Accompanying lectures: *Mystery Knowledge and Mystery Centres* (CW 232); *World History in the Light of Anthroposophy* (CW 233). December 25: the Foundation Stone is laid (in the hearts of members) in the form of the 'Foundation Stone Meditation.'

1924: January 1: having founded the Anthroposophical Society and taken over its leadership, Rudolf Steiner has the task of 'reforming' it. The process begins with a weekly newssheet ('What's Happening in the Anthroposophical Society') in which Rudolf Steiner's 'Letters to Members' and 'Anthroposophical Leading Thoughts' appear (CW 26). The next step is the creation of a new esoteric class, the 'first class' of the 'University of Spiritual Science' (which was to have been followed, had Rudolf Steiner lived longer, by two more advanced classes). Then comes a new language for Anthroposophy—practical, phenomenological, and direct; and Rudolf Steiner creates the model for the second Goetheanum. He begins the series of extensive 'karma' lectures (CW 235–40); and finally, responding to needs, he creates two new initiatives: biodynamic agriculture and curative education. After the middle of the year, rumours begin to circulate regarding Steiner's health. Lectures: January–February, *Anthroposophy* (CW 234); February: *Tone Eurythmy* (CW 278); June: *The Agriculture Course* (CW 327); June–July: *Speech Eurythmy* (CW 279); *Curative Education* (CW 317); August: (England, 'Second International Summer School'), *Initiation Consciousness: True and False Paths in Spiritual Investigation* (CW 243); September: *Pastoral Medicine* (CW 318). On September 26, for the first time, Rudolf Steiner cancels a lecture. On September 28, he gives his last lecture. On September 29, he withdraws to his studio in the carpenter's shop; now he is definitively ill. Cared for by Ita Wegman, he continues working, however, and writing the weekly installments of his *Autobiography* and *Letters to the Members/Leading Thoughts* (CW 26).

1925: Rudolf Steiner, while continuing to work, continues to weaken. He finishes *Extending Practical Medicine* (CW 27) with Ita Wegman.

On March 30, around ten in the morning, Rudolf Steiner dies.

INDEX